ORIGAMI ART

15 Exquisite Folded Paper Designs from the Origamido Studio

Michael G. LaFosse

Richard L. Alexander

TUTTLE PUBLISHING
Tokyo • Rutland, Vermont • Singapore

CONTENTS

Facing page: Butterflies in handmade, Origamido™ duo papers were displayed and sold on several fabric walls using removable Velcro™ dots, which also allowed them to be worn on clothing, affixed to curtains, or changeable picture frames.

INTRODUCTION

By Richard Alexander

An article was published in a 1970 *Reader's Digest* about Akira Yoshizawa, an inspired paper-folding artist from Tokyo. Thirty-two years earlier, at the age of 26, he had quit his job at an iron foundry, and decided to devote the rest of his life to creating origami art. Michael LaFosse was a fourteen-year-old living in Fitchburg, Massachusetts when he first saw that article with compelling photos of Yoshizawa's remarkable, lifelike creations. As he read intently about this whole new world of origami art, Michael decided he too would be an origami artist.

What Michael and Yoshizawa had in common was a fascination for transforming a single square piece of paper into something wonderful. Each had been captivated at an early age by their ability to express artistic creativity through the process of folding paper. Each had been frustrated by the simplicity of the traditional models. They wanted more. The article mentioned that Yoshizawa dreamed of establishing a museum and research center to extend the benefits of origami to the world. In 1996, Michael and I opened the Origamido Studio to the public to do just that.

The earliest documented process for making paper was developed in China in the second century A.D. Paper folding possibly spread with paper along the trade routes to Japan and Europe, models being taught by one person to another. Early folded designs were surely utilitarian, then ceremonial. Paper-folding designs practiced in Europe and Asia probably resulted from alternating periods of sharing, then isolation with considerable independent development. Until the Industrial Revolution, paper was likely too precious to be folded for fun. Until the communications revolution, and for nearly two thousand years, the complexity of the folded paper designs was limited by the teacher's ability to pass on the various folding sequences.

Yoshizawa had only six years of formal schooling, but his school years occurred when the world was being swept by a new educational curriculum for young children, originally developed by a German named Friedrich Froebel. His "Kindergarten" incorporated the exercises of folding paper squares into different shapes and patterns as an educational tool. Scholars credit the current, international use of the word "Origami" to the translation of the words "Papier Falten" (paper folding) from German Kindergarten textbooks, introduced to Japan around 1900. Scholars credit the export of the Froebellian Kindergarten system to Japan, and the subsequent translation of instructions for teachers, for the beginning of the current, international use of the Japanese word, "Origami." The traditional Japanese paper folding repertoire, before the time of Yoshizawa, probably numbered fewer than 100 models. Until the introduction of Kindergarten in Japan, paper folding was essentially relegated to the crafting realm of grandmothers and their granddaughters. The formalization of paper folding in elementary schools, thanks to their adoption of the European system, helped legitimize and broaden the Japanese understanding of this craft as a useful learning tool, and not just a trivial pastime.

Facing page: "Dancing Cranes," Alexander's modern, spinning composition.

Above left: Akira Yoshizawa in his Tokyo studio, holding his Origami Gorilla.

Above right: Origamido Studio on Wingate Street, Haverhill, Massachusetts.

Kindergarten seems to have spurred the Japanese to revisit and further explore their traditional and ceremonial folded paper models, embracing paper crafts with more excitement than the Kindergartens of the USA or Europe. Along with Kindergarten came inexpensive, mass-produced squares of colored folding papers. Until Yoshizawa, folding paper was considered a Kindergarten craft and pastime. By the time the *Reader's Digest* article was written, Yoshizawa was 58 years old and claimed to have created and saved some 20,000 origami models in his house. Some would say that he alone has been responsible for the birth of a true and significant folk art.

Yoshizawa claims to have never sold a piece, being so passionately involved in their creation, he considered his origami models as "his children." Both Michael and I have traveled to Tokyo and watched Yoshizawa retrieve, unwrap, contemplate, then re-wrap and store dozens of his favorite pieces. It was easy to see why he did not sell those breathtaking works, not only because they were "his children," but because they represented so much work and personal, emotional investment, that no price was ever high enough. Even the simplest models clearly showed the artist's touch—the unique magic of paper art.

We want the Origamido Studio to help develop a deeper understanding, and hence, a better appreciation for this new art—to help people understand why certain models are significant, perhaps because of their technology, history, development, and provenance; but also because of their elegant beauty, and how through them, the artist is able to speak to our souls.

Origami art as a recent development is indeed a strange type of art. Imagine Rembrandt writing a book about how to paint a dozen of his luminescent masterpieces. Or imagine Michelangelo recording a video about how to carve his glorious Pieta. At the Origamido Studio, Michael has often used the analogy of music to explain that the art of origami not only requires the designer (composer), but talented and skilled folders (musicians), using the most superb instruments (handmade paper), and practiced technique. In this light, we offer this additional set of diagrammed projects for yet more complex origami art models requiring advanced folding skill sets, and of course, an artist's vision.

Our first hardcover book devoted solely to origami art, *Origamido: Masterworks in Folded Paper* (Rockport Publishers) was primarily a book of photos of a spectrum of contemporary origami models by forty international living masters. As such, it was the first of its kind—a coffee table book serving as an origami art exhibit between boards.

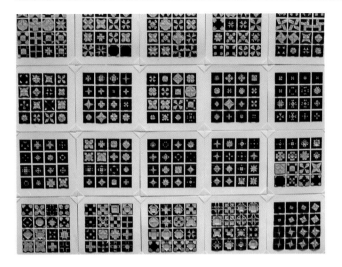

Michael had coined the word Origamido when he was a teenager, to distinguish the art of origami represented by Yoshizawa's amazing work from the pastime of simple folded paper amusements. *Ori* is from oru, meaning to fold; *gami* from kami, meaning paper; and the suffix *do* referring to the way, path, experience or journey of following a prescribed discipline.

Many of the models shown in *Origamido: Masterworks* had been only recently displayed at a special exhibition at the Carousel du Louvre, in Paris. Until then, only a relatively few origami aficionados attending conventions saw these works up close and in person. The *Origamido: Masterworks* book brought exquisite origami art to thousands. Several of these artworks also went on display at the Mingei museum in San Diego, thanks to the dedication and hard work of V'Ann Cornelius and others. The show was so popular, it was extended, and another version of the show was set up for an additional stay in a satellite facility.

When we published some of Michael's designs in the *Advanced Origami* book (Tuttle Publishing) a few of years later, it not only revealed in detail how such masterworks were actually folded, it contained information about how special papers were made by hand, in addition to complete folding diagrams.

This book continues the offerings of our previously published, advanced books and video lessons. It is for the growing number of intermediate to super-complex paper folders, inspired by the exhibition of spectacular origami on the Internet, at conventions, and in places like the Origamido Studio.

Clockwise from top left:
Friedrich Froebel's Kindergarten patterns of folded papers.

Traditional Senbazuru of Three Connected Cranes. Folded by Greg Mudarri.

Akira Yoshizawa's origami birds.

Traditional Japanese Ceremonial Noshi folded by Greg Mudarri.

THE HISTORY OF THE ORIGAMIDO STUDIO

By Richard Alexander

Michael LaFosse and I co-founded the Origamido Studio in 1996. We met in 1988, when Michael was an Executive Chef and I was an environmental regulations consultant. We shared several interests, including SCUBA diving, science, history, art, and aviation. During our first meeting, Michael opened his shoeboxes of origami, and I was astounded. His models were exquisitely folded in the highest detail, from papers the likes of which I had never seen. He told me that he made his own papers, so he could avoid the eventual deterioration from the internal acids found in most commercial papers.

I consider origami to be perhaps the most unique of folk arts. After graduating from Cornell, I had lived in New York City from 1975 to 1980, and had the pleasure of spending time at the Metropolitan Museum of Art. The Director at the time was Thomas Hoving, a dynamic force in the New York art world, and I was thrilled to hear him speak about art in a lecture given at the Rockefeller University, where I was living.

Hoving defined art as works of impeccable quality that people wanted to save, cherish, and possess. The first cave-art critic that said "That one's good. Let's not draw over it." set things in motion. This is how I felt about Michael's origami Big Brown Bat. I told him that seeing his art squirreled away in boxes reminded me of the Bible parable of the candlelight being hidden under a bushel basket. I said "Let's not only save it, let's show it to the world."

My work since 1975 had involved designing environmental protection programs tailored to the manufacturing industry, and I had been documenting best practices for water conservation, wastewater and hazardous waste minimization, using videotape since 1980. I asked Michael if his work had been documented on video, and he dismissed the idea, explaining that people learned origami from books. He showed me booklets of his diagrams for folding an origami airplane, the F-14 Tomcat, that he had offered for sale through an ad in the back of *Popular Science Magazine*.

He thought that origami video had not been done, but later recalled that his first introduction to origami was from a PBS (Public Broadcasting Service) show he caught while being at home from school during a sick day. The Japanese host showed the audience how to fold the origami Waterbomb (balloon, or box), repeating the lesson several times. Michael memorized it, and he was hooked.

ARTISTIC AWAKENING

Michael's uncle introduced him to origami paper airplanes, and his grandmother kept him busy making things from paper. As described in the introduction, Michael was fascinated with origami from an early age, and was awakened to the artistic potential of origami through that famed *Reader's Digest* article about the works of Akira Yoshizawa, published in 1970.

Facing page: Alexander's "origami-esque" Paper People for print ad campaign for SmartPage™ Technologies.

Clockwise from top left:
Traditional Water Bomb, or Balloon.

LaFosse's Origami F-14 Tomcat
Fighter Paper Airplane.

LaFosse's Origami Cattleya Orchid
from the *Advanced Origami* book
(Tuttle Publishing).

LaFosse's origami Big Brown Bat
from the *Advanced Origami* book
(Tuttle Publishing).

Michael could neither locate, nor afford papers of exactly the right types, colors, textures, sizes and finishes for the complex origami designs he had in mind. This spurred a period of experimentation with making papers by hand. Fortunately, he lived in Fitchburg, Massachusetts, a papermaking town, and Michael was able to glean the answers to his technical questions from libraries and paper factory personnel.

Paper for origami art has to be archival, so it must be colored with inorganic pigments, not dyes, and it often has to be large, strong and thin. Soon, he learned to control the paper's properties by carefully selecting the source and species of fibers, beating them to the proper condition, experimenting with blends of different fibers, controlling the chemistry (selecting and developing recipes for adding just the right amounts of formation aids, retention aids, size and pigments) and choosing the correct sheet forming, pressing, and drying techniques.

Along with these stronger, thinner papers came his ability to create more complex origami designs heretofore not seen. These papers allowed him to fold his intricate Praying Mantis, Cattleya Orchid, and Big Brown Bat. He also found that creating just the right paper for an origami project could sometimes be more frustrating and challenging than actually folding the piece.

NEW YORK CITY, THE ORIGAMI HOTBED

Despite Michael's visits to Lillian Oppenheimer's Origami Center of America in New York City back in 1976 and 1977, he had been folding essentially in isolation for several years—common practice before the birth of the World Wide Web. Certain prominent personalities of the New York origami scene in the 1970s were dismissive of Michael's art, claiming that it was paper sculpture and not origami at all. This drove Michael back into folding in relative isolation. For a while he lived in Williamstown, Massachusetts, where he was able to make handmade papers. When I met him in 1988, he was living in Chelmsford, Massachusetts, and his apartment was too small for papermaking. I had just built my house on the Merrimack River. Michael moved in, and we had plenty of room to make art.

In 1991, Michael re-connected with the Origami enthusiasts he had visited nearly twenty years before. He found out there would soon be an opportunity to meet the man who folded the magnificent origami art featured in a *Reader's Digest* article from 1970. We drove to Ossining, NY so Michael could attend a master class workshop being given by Akira Yoshizawa of Tokyo. It was here that Michael developed a strong relationship with him through another of Yoshizawa's students, Emiko Kruckner. (Kruckner had studied with Yoshizawa in Japan, and was living in New Jersey at the time.) During the class, Michael felt a sense of validation from Yoshizawa, who gave Michael high praise for his artful folding. I could see that Michael had the right combination of folding skill, experience, and artistic sensibilities to advance the art of paper folding into the mainstream art world.

Portable oak pedestals constructed with hinged bases in 1992, as set up in Origamido Studio, 2005.

BOSTON, THE ORIGAMI OUTPOST

Once again, Michael began making paper at home. Without sophisticated, expensive equipment for pressing the paper, we stacked plywood on the wet pulp and parked our pickup truck on top. Always in search of signs of advanced origami in the Boston area, we came across Anthony Matosich, folding origami jewelry for sale from a push-cart at Faneuil Hall Marketplace. (Come to find out, Tony grew up in Ithaca, just 12 miles from where I did in the Finger Lakes Region of upstate New York. He had folded an origami baby grand piano, designed by Patricia Crawford, on the Gymnasium floor at the Ithaca High School.) Tony narrated a video I shot with Michael folding some basic origami models, and sold 100 copies at Faneuil Hall.

The Friends of the Origami Center of America (FOCA), held their Annual Convention in June of 1992 at an elementary school on the Upper West Side of Manhattan. Rather than take dozens of origami models, we selected only his seven strongest pieces. Each piece was shown under a custom acrylic bonnet, on an oak pedestal. The unique method of display garnered additional attention for the models, and encouraged people to examine each piece more carefully.

OFF AND RUNNING

Kyoko Kondo, an origami aficionado, and volunteer at FOCA, called Michael in 1993, to see if he could fold origami for Saks Fifth Avenue's retail store windows. This was the start of our folding a series of four sets of origami displays for Saks. His Happy Good-Luck Bats were selected for Halloween windows in October, then we folded hundreds of origami tulips and butterflies in February for their Spring collection. The butterflies were so popular, we folded more, larger butterflies and large, multi-piece flowers and leaves that summer; then returned in the autumn with boxes full of falling leaves, folded in pleated black and silver paper, offset by white, hyperbolic torchiere lamps, and paper shirts.

These commissions were our introduction to the fast-paced world of commercial art design and production. The first request came on a Wednesday. The customer needed concept sketches on Thursday. They gave us the green light on Friday. We called our friends, procured the right papers and folded hundreds of origami elements on the weekend, so Michael could fly to New York City aboard the first flight on Monday. Working with the Saks team, they installed the folded art in ten huge windows by sundown, Monday, and Michael flew back to Boston that evening.

EXPANDING HORIZONS

The origami windows at Saks created quite a buzz, and other designers asked if we had patterns for the paper art. Rockport Publishers had worked with Michael to put together a hardcover book called *Paper Art: The Art of Sculpting with Paper* (Quarry Books). The next year, Michael put together a set of cut, fold and paste (paper craft) books in their Make It With Paper series. The titles included *Paper Flowers*, *Paper Animals*, and *Paper Boxes*. He also drew the illustrations for *Paper Pop-Ups* authored by fellow origami artist, Paul Jackson, from England (now living in Israel). These books featured tear-out, printed sheets that enabled the reader to replicate the projects shown on the front cover. They also contained shape templates that window designers could enlarge (or reduce) to generate similar flowers, animals and boxes in any size or material.

Below: LaFosse's Butterflies and Alexander's Tulips in Springtime window displays at Saks Fifth Avenue, New York City.

Bottom: LaFosse's Summer Flowers window at Saks Fifth Avenue, New York City.

An exhibit company working for the United Nations asked us to design and construct an 11-foot tall tree with removable branches fitted with hundreds of origami leaves. The tree accompanied a UNICEF show explaining the importance of their Rights of the Children initiative, and traveled through ten cities in Japan in 1994. This was not just a folding job. The tree itself required considerable thought and engineering, careful selection of materials, hardware, and components. It required us to purchase or borrow special tools and to find people with the talents we lacked.

Later that year, Michael was offered a one-man show of his original origami art at Lasell College (Yamawaki Center) in Newton, Massachusetts. He showed his best work in a beautiful setting, and incorporated a community exhibit (the mock-up we made for the UNICEF tree) so attendees could fold an origami model and hang it on a branch. Michael made dozens of contacts at the show, and was able to speak with several teachers about incorporating origami into the classroom. He had become a full-time origami artist while teaching visitors attending the show.

When the show came down, Michael scheduled more programs at local schools, museums and libraries. When not busy teaching, we taped more video lessons, including his Happy Good-Luck Bats and Horseshoe Crab. This videocassette also featured a tour of the origami art show at Lasell College. By then, we had videotaped many of his models, including the F-14 Tomcat and several of his other great paper airplanes. Later that year, we also published Michael's video lessons for his Origami Penguin and Squirrel, as well as his lessons for his Origami Sea Turtle and Koi. There seemed to be nothing similar that showed how an origami master wet-folds these realistic, 3-D models, and there was a growing market for this information.

Origami designer and computer guru, Jay Nolan, had been on the cutting edge of computer drawing programs, and asked Michael's permission to diagram some of his works, directly from watching the video instructions. Jay's diagrams appeared in the FOCA compendiums, and set the standard for others drawing origami instructions. In 1995, we published Jay's book, *Creating Origami*, which helped answer the universal question posed to every origami designer, "How did you come up with that model?" We followed up with the publication of Jay's drawings in *Awesome Origami* volumes I and II. Jay has been a great friend and origami art collector of Michael's work.

Above left: LaFosse's Halloween windows at Saks Fifth Avenue, New York City.

Above right: LaFosse's silver and black leaves, Alexander's hyperbolic torch in Autumn windows at Saks Fifth Avenue, New York City.

Below: Origami Tree for UNICEF; a close-up of the leaves.

Above left: LaFosse's Horseshoe Crab.

Above right: LaFosse's Happy Good Luck Bats.

Right: Great white shark designed for a print ad camaign for Pfizer, Inc.

Later that year, we were contacted by the Union Camp paper company's ad agency to produce origami to kick off a marketing campaign for their Great White™, office bond from recycled fiber. The event was held at the New England Aquarium. They commissioned Michael to design a great white shark. Larger versions of the sharks decorated each of the tables on the patio for the lobster bake. Smaller versions of the design, packaged in jewelry boxes, were presented to each of the 500 paper merchants assembled for the kickoff celebration. This shark design came in handy several years later, when Pfizer needed aggressive animals to market their aggressive antibiotic, Zithromax™. Michael folded origami props for a scripted performance that described the importance of recycling paper to keep nature in balance. Michael was called back to the Aquarium to fold penguins with spectators at the opening of an expanded, live penguin exhibit.

THE BIRTH OF THE ORIGAMIDO STUDIO

There was an opening on the Mayor's Arts Commission, and Michael was tapped in 1996 to help decide how to fund the local arts activities and events. He urged me to attend a public input meeting. Chairman Peter Waldron mused something like "Isn't there a way we could set up an arts center downtown to help the local artists by giving them a place to work and show their art?" The Pentucket Arts Center was born from that idea, and Michael and I were soon on a committee to search for and select a suitable physical location.

We explored several vacant storefronts, and met with a young man who had recently purchased an old brick shoe factory at auction, located less than a half block from the downtown train station. His goal was to fill his vacant building, and our goal was to find affordable, centrally-located space. I gave the building owner a check to lease the corner storefront for the Origamido Studio. Within a month, our commitment had convinced the Pentucket Arts Center Board of Directors to lease the space next door. Soon, restaurants and other galleries opened on Wingate Street, and we had an interesting collection of arts-related businesses in the downtown district.

We designed a sign that listed the products and services we would provide:

- Art
- Exhibits
- Workshops
- Publications

- Design
- Video
- Instruction
- Installations

During the next 11 years, Origamido Studio became synonymous with compelling exhibits, powerful art for the discerning collector, great new designs that are fun to fold, effective and unique advertising, "edutainment"—lectures, presentations, programs of instruction by origami experts, and nearly 50 publications (books, videos and kits) designed to satisfy paper folders at all levels. Curious people were able to walk in off the street, learn about origami, and take a short lesson.

As soon as we signed the lease, we got a call from a marketing agent whose granddaughter suggested he develop an origami kit for QVC, the TV shopping channel. We proposed to shoot a 1-hour videocassette, and package it with paper so that people could enjoy some traditional origami without the struggle of following technical diagrams. This was our first mass-market product, and we were off and running.

IMPACTING THE WORLD OF ORIGAMI

We did not realize when we started that the Origamido Studio would make significant contributions to the world of paper folding. Since the smallest batch of handmade paper for each of Michael's fine art models made about a hundred sheets, there was plenty of extra paper that we made available to other advanced origami artists.

The Studio became well known as a place for accomplished origami artists and authors to come to collaborate on projects, whether they involved publishing, advertising, art, videos, or exhibits. The Studio's commercial work brought origami designs to the public, and exposed the art to a worldwide audience. Our video lessons were broadcast on local public access television, as well as at large, public events, such as fairs, conventions, and at Symphony Hall. We developed hundreds of new models, and expanded the repertoire of origami taught through Story-gami, a technique used to entertain while teaching. These stories generated unforgettable visuals, and often silly images, while the story itself linked the folding steps in a logical sequence. Our simple dollar bill folds presented on DVD have become popular entry-level models for people to fold while waiting for anything.

Our papermaking workshops have enabled origami artists to raise the level of their art. During a recent show and sale of high-end origami art in Vancouver, Canada, a surprising number of the pieces were wet-folded from Origamido Studio paper.

Top: Origamido Studio's first product for sale on QVC, 1997.

Above: Origami Artist, Jason Ku, selecting Origamido™ handmade papers.

Above right: Alexander and class at Origami Studio.

Robert Lang, famed origami designer, folder and author, has observed that the higher quality and strength of the Origamido™ hand-made papers has allowed origami creators to actually fold some of their super-complex models that weren't possible to fold from previously available papers. Now they could finally realize their origami ambitions. It is a two-way street. These more inspiring, complex and super-complex designs have kept the pressure on us to make even better, stronger, more uniform papers from innovative fiber blends.

A DEDICATED SPACE FOR DIVERSE PROJECTS

Despite the fact that we were busy, we seemed to be doing a little of everything. There was no established origami business model, and we found ourselves reacting to the needs of the next caller. From January through June each year, Michael drove to the regional schools, libraries, colleges, and museums to teach origami and to display selected masterworks from our studio.

We also performed occasional origami lectures, demonstrations and workshops for several corporations. One of my favorite challenges was to fold origami footwear in an impromptu setting with the designers at Reebok/Rockport Shoe Headquarters in Canton, Massachusetts. We were thrilled to address technical groups, such as dentists and their families at the Yankee Dental Conference. Michael addressed the

International Puzzle Conference at the Logan Airport Hilton. We also conducted several teachers' conferences, and used the *Paper Art* book as a syllabus for teaching groups of art teachers through the University of Connecticut. Michael made the drive every Easter weekend to teach origami to in Greenwich Connecticut.

After we developed an Internet site during 1996, several advertisers found us and the opportunities snowballed from there. What was originally a luxury of having a separate, dedicated space for the origami business had become essential, and made these disparate jobs even possible. So many projects have been nurtured in the Origamido Studio that it's impossible to list them all in this short space, but just a sampling of the highlights include the following.

- A TV commercial for McDonald's Restaurants (What can you do with a couple of bucks?). We folded dollars into a dozen different shapes, including: a biplane, the Eiffel Tower, an aardvark, a push-me-pull-you, a space shuttle, and a McDonald's restaurant.

- Various TV commercials, including a Jumbo Jet from lined school paper for a ToySmart™ spot, and Paul Revere's house for a Columbo Yogurt spot.

Top: Cut, fold and paste Jumbo Jet Prop for a ToySmart™ TV Commercial.

Right: LaFosse with pleated tube prototype for space use.

■ Workshops and exhibitions focusing on natural history subjects at the Cape Cod Museum of Natural History. Models included: grackle, goldfish, horseshoe crabs, big brown bat, Wilbur the piglet, sea turtles, a pond turtle, and manatees.

■ Exhibitions at the Cahoon Museum of American Art in Cotuit, Massachusetts and at the Art Complex of Duxbury, Massachusetts, with other origami artists invited to send their works.

■ The design of pleating patterns for a high tech applications, including space-going heat and dust shields, shipboard equipment, and clean room apparatus.

■ The design of about 24 origami renditions of the creatures of the Sonoran Desert after an internship with the Arizona-Sonora Desert Museum, including: a giant hairy scorpion, a roadrunner, coyote family, a mask of the ASDM mascot (George L. Mountainlion), Hummingbirds, butterflies, squirrel, frog, rattlesnake, prairie dog, mice, praying mantis, and a Harris Hawk.

■ During October of 2001, one of Japan's most gifted origami talents, Satoshi Kamiya, began a ten-month papermaking internship at the Origamido Studio. This gave us an opportunity to formulate new recipes and different

Top left: LaFosse's Origami Harris Hawk.

Top right: LaFosse's Origami Frog in handmade, Origamido™ paper.

Above: LaFosse's Origami American Alligator in handmade Origamido™ paper.

blends of handmade papers more appropriate for the super-complex models that Satoshi had been developing. He and Michael designed and made batches of special papers for his blue whale, wasp, beetles, phoenix, pegasus, grasshopper, night stalker, archaeopteryx, coelophysis, orca, sea turtle, wizard, sparrow, and pterodactyl.

- Hermes of Paris placed an order for monumental origami to grace seven store windows to feature their new watch. The largest piece was to be an eight foot tall Pegasus with front hoof raised to sport the timepiece. It took three weeks to build the piece, and because of transportation concerns, it had to be constructed from several sheets of folded watercolor paper. The structural support had to be completely hidden, so three upright pipes through the legs supported the sculpture.

- We were hired to create paper props for a print ad campaign. The client wanted a series of objects that corporations typically invested in when they became profitable, including a copy machine, telephone system, computers, a company car, new office furniture, and enthusiastic new employees. These were to be origami-esque constructions from white paper.

- In a show called FLorigami, featuring threatened and endangered creatures from South Florida and the Everglades, Michael folded at least two dozen origami models, folded from paper we made by hand at the Origamido Studio. The series of green and brown tinted sheets resulted from a 20-day paper-making marathon. I made three enormous sheets of greenish-gray paper for Michael's American Alligator.

During all of these events, exhibits, and publications, the Origamido Studio was open for folding classes and parties. We held Beginners' Walk-In Folding Night every Thursday between 6 and 8 p.m. So many people kept coming back, even though they thoroughly knew the beginner's repertoire, we added a walk-in night for intermediate level folders on Fridays. The classes were free for customers that purchased at least $20 of supplies that evening. During the holiday season, we also held product-focused folding workshops each Wednesday, so people interested in cards, boxes, gift wrapping, ornaments or other topical models could purchase a book or kit, and use it the same night to work through any questions about the projects it contained.

Having a place large enough for groups of people to work together, with all the required resources of paper, tables, and an extensive origami research library made it possible to bring the joy of origami to the community in such an engaging manner.

LOOKING FORWARD

After completing ten years at the Wingate Street location, Michael and I decided to move the business to Hawaii. Hawaii's Aloha spirit and Asian sensibilities seemed to be a better fit for what we wanted to do. The move would be a radical shift from life in New England, but artists often need change, and this would promise to be stimulating. My cousin had lived in Hawaii for nearly 30 years, and I felt that a warmer climate was in our future.

Facing page: Pegasus (eight feet tall) for Hermes of Paris, New York City. The response after installation was heartwarming; "It stopped traffic on Madison Avenue!" That double take is what every advertiser is paying for.

Realizing fully well that it could take considerable time to plan and execute the move, we wanted the best origami art from our gallery to continue to be seen by the public while we made the physical move. As we closed and packed the Wingate Street facility, the art from our gallery was installed at the Peabody Essex Museum, and the Fitchburg Art Museum. The high attendance numbers and positive feedback from these shows has allowed us to re-evaluate how our next location should function.

The simultaneous maturation of the Internet has revolutionized origami learning, particularly through video. The Peabody Essex Museum show dedicated their Media Center to video origami lessons. Comcast cable TV was a major sponsor, and even people without the Comcast On Demand service were able to log onto the PEM.org website, or the activityTV.tv websites to take advantage of our free, video instructions for beginners. Thousands of people each week were not only exposed to the most remarkable origami masterworks for inspiration, they were able to fold several projects themselves, folding while learning at their own pace by pausing or replaying the video clips.

For years, people urged us to franchise the Origamido Studio, but we could not imagine how others could quickly develop the skill set that it took Michael dozens of years to hone. We had always used any extra cash to advertise, and never thought the level of cash flow would interest potential franchisees. These exhibits indicated that a large show with high value exhibits and properly integrated interactivity seemed to be a viable "edutainment" business. More importantly, these shows were able to process busloads of visitors—something that the Origamido Studio could not have done.

Opposite: FUGU, designed and folded by Sipho Mabona, Switzerland, from a single square of Origamido™ paper.

Below: Origami wasp in handmade, Origamido™ paper by Satoshi Kamiya at the Origamido Studio.

DESIGNING ORIGAMI ART FOR DISPLAY

By Richard Alexander

Most of the origami we learned in elementary school was suitable for pasting on a greeting card. Much of the early origami repertoire was merely a silhouette resembling the shape of a familiar object or animal. It was easy when there was only one view to consider. Things have certainly changed. Origami art designed for public display may carry special design criteria. Now we entertain somewhat bizarre needs for origami art, certainly in commercial settings. Perhaps the origami display must involve motion. Either it must move, or perhaps it must be engaging to people in moving autos. Perhaps it must have pleasing shapes and shadows when backlit, as suspended from a 40-foot glassed-in atrium. This chapter will address the aspects we consider when designing a piece of origami art for public installation. We will discuss the importance of subject choice, composition, views and viewing angles, command of the space, and the relationships of the origami art model to other models, or to the surroundings.

SUBJECT CHOICE

Origami art designed for public display must engage the sensibilities of the viewer. The artist may want to excite, please, or even startle the viewer, such as our origami bats in the store windows with haute couture fashion mannequins at Saks Fifth Avenue. The fact is that there still are some people who are repulsed by bats, and the old wives' tales of bats becoming entangled in your hair persist. Even publishers fall prey to common misperceptions about natural history subjects, and we had a hard time convincing this publisher not to refer to Michael's bat featured on the *Advanced Origami* book jacket as a Frightening Bat! Both Michael and I had worked with bats in college, and want to spread respect and knowledge about the beneficial aspects of bats. They pollinate. They keep the mosquito population in check. They are fascinating creatures considered symbols of good luck and fortune in Asia.

Sometimes the subject is not as important as the material. I observed earlier that young children are drawn to origami folded from money.

COMPOSITION

Michael and I drove to an origami convention in Seattle (a 6,000 mile round trip), and when we arrived, we toured the city with other origami masters gathered from around the world. Hojyo Takashi, of Japan, whipped out his camera to photograph nearly every piece of sculpture on the tour. I asked him why he was so interested in Seattle's statues. He explained that for him, the composition of an origami piece was the most challenging aspect. Should he decide to create an origami version of a famous bronze figure, he could rest assured that the "hard work" of composition was already done. The folding design, for him, was easy compared to the overall composition.

Facing page: Compound origami plant with butterfly, in handmade Origamido™ paper. Each element is from a single square. The elements are assembled on paper-covered wire.

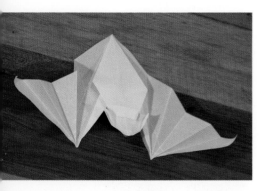

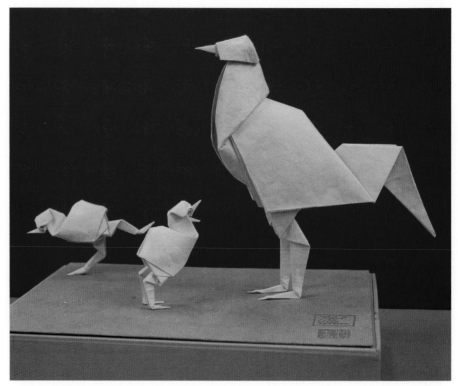

Top: LaFosse's Abstract became his Happy Good-Luck Bat design.

Above: LaFosse's Happy Good-Luck Bats, a design developed for commercial advertising.

Above right: "Origami Hen and Chicks," designed by Akira Yoshizawa and folded by Michael LaFosse. Both the sensitive shaping of the origami and their compositional relationship enhance the viewer's appreciation when on display together.

Angle of View

I understood Hojyo's sentiments completely. Even my earliest art training in grade school challenged me to consider turning the owl's head on the piece I was carving from a mixture of vermiculite and Plaster of Paris. Ms. Vorce insisted that the sculpture be interesting from every angle of view, even though there may be a primary angle of view. Proportion, balance, negative space, light and dark—these are the tough compromises all artists must make that constitute the "hard work" that Hojyo spoke of. Will the piece be mounted into a shadowbox for the wall? Is it being designed for a niche in the hallway? Will it occupy a glass case or dust bonnet in a museum? Will people see it from above when they descend a stairway or escalator?

Command of Space

This can be difficult for origami, because models are traditionally quite small. The problem is not just obtaining large paper, it is in dealing with structural limitations when folding paper that may be 20, 30, or 40 feet square. Gravity can make even an exquisitely folded Japanese Crane seem clunky, floppy, and awkward, even when it is actually smaller than a life-size crane! For any material or type of paper, there is an optimum size for the origami. Few models better illustrate this point than Valerie Vann's elaborate Magic Rose Cube.

Too small, and it begins to look inconsequential. The manipulation of the miniscule facets with one's thumbs and fingertips to transform the cube into a flower could also be incredibly difficult with particularly small models. On the other hand, a massive Magic Rose Cube folded from extra large paper seems to be an affront to our sensibilities. Valerie recommends using paper between three and five inches square—a tight window for an origami model. We wanted to use this model for a floral display in our own gallery windows, but the models needed to be larger than is recommended. The solution was to affix the large rose cubes onto an even larger, geometric trellis.

Above left: Origamido Mobile of origami-esque Common Terns and Gulls, Tom Ridge Environmental Center, Erie, Pennsylvania.

Above right: Origami "God of Thunder" by Hojyo on public display at the HSBC Bank lobby, Vancouver, B.C. during P.C.O.C., Pacific Coast Origami Conference, 2007.

We often overcome the Command of Space issue by increasing the number of objects, or by developing relationships between origami objects. Elsa Chen and Aimee Miura enjoyed their individual origami animals after attending a Joseph Wu workshop in Seattle, but soon discovered that the pair of models seemed to belong together, so that is how they displayed them—patty-cake style, in the same display case. All of a sudden, the juxtaposition of the two objects changed the message, and the public reacted! We recalled that experience when we displayed these complimentary Wu creations at the Fitchburg Art Museum in 2007.

One of the first sets of commercial window displays that we designed origami for was at the Manhattan Saks Fifth Avenue store. Michael was troubled by the challenge of installing original origami for twelve huge windows—several along Fifth Avenue opposite the promenade to Rockefeller Center. We were sitting in our living room when the idea came to mind of using one design, repeated multiple times. The solution was hanging over Michael's head.

He had discarded a pleated piece of white, translucent paper, which I thought looked like an abstract bat. Halloween was coming up, and I asked him to pitch the idea of folding origami bats to surround the mannequins featuring the haute couture fashions. Reluctantly, he discussed the idea, and soon he perfected the folding pattern of what is now known as his Happy, Good-Luck Bat. Not only did he mount several nestled tightly in the corners of the windows as groupings of roosting bats (the power of multiple elements), some appeared to be swooping through the space (conjures motion) while others were menacing the mannequin's heels (startling relationship). The public did a double take—exactly what the art director was looking for. The small bats totally commanded the space!

The Tom Ridge Environmental Center at Presque Isle (Erie, PA) is the permanent home to some 70 origami or "origami-esque" birds (13 species in all) that Michael folded in watercolor paper.

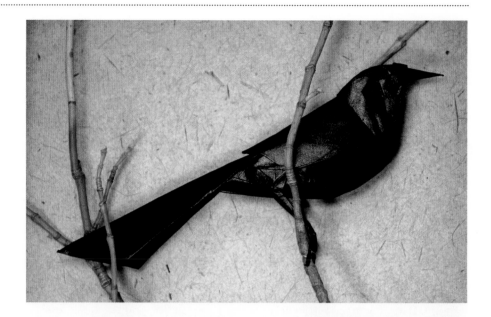

Top: Contextual display, showing Origami Grackle in real branches.

Right: LaFosse's Origami Rattlesnake for the Arizona Sonora Desert Museum, Tucson, Arizona.

The contract called for us to design and install five large mobiles, and several other static displays. Each arm of the mobiles was fixed to two or three of the paper birds. Watercolor paper allowed us to add splashes of color to conjure the depicted species. Whether the mobiles were vertical (such as the 15 foot tall stainless steel double helix with turkey vultures and harriers), or horizontal, (such as the 12 foot wide, cluster of common terns and ring-billed gulls) the spatial relationships change as the mobiles turn. Another stainless steel support resembles a bush. The outer branches swing around the center trunk. Red-eyed vireos share the bush with a pair of woodcocks. Although each mobile was different in shape and motion, each was formed from similar, stainless steel rods and connecting swivels. Each origami model was repeated in different poses to form related groupings. Groups of two or more species were arranged on the mobiles to depict their natural interactive relationship. The Grand Opening was Memorial Day, 2006.

Relationship to Surroundings

On the most basic level, origami art on display must relate to its surroundings. For years, people have posed their origami art in contextually appropriate settings. We have photographed an origami seal on a real rock, an origami squirrel next to real oak leaves, and even an origami grackle on a real branch.

When Michael and I met the other Directors of Origami USA to go through the overly-packed storage space in the bowels of the American Museum of Natural History in New York City, some of the largest pieces in storage were origami dioramas, perhaps five or six feet on each side, depicting life in Central Park during different seasons. Origami animals were posed among origami flowers, trees, ponds, bridges, and lampposts. Admittedly, the tendency to do this is quite popular. A contextual relationship need not be so immediately obvious. For instance, when we installed the display of Michael's origami renditions of desert animals and plants at the Ironwood Gallery of the Arizona-Sonora Desert Museum, one of the connections that was not immediately apparent was that the subjects were folded of handmade paper consisting of desert plant fiber. The majority of the pieces on display were paired according to the real-life relationships of the subjects: The origami rattlesnake in the upper showcase was heading for the lower showcase containing a pair of origami mice.

Similarly, the coyote was presented near the roadrunner, origami butterflies on a scientifically accurate origami rendition of milkweed; black-chinned origami hummingbirds mounted to blossoms on a jacobina sprig. In each case, the contextual setting and/or relationship of the origami art enhanced the viewers' enjoyment. Other themes also help establish a relationship between origami subjects, such as a grouping of "forgotten polinators" (bats, birds and butterflies).

Above left: Origami Metamorphosis, showing interrelation of objects on display, one form becomes the next, engaging the viewer.

Above right: Valerie Vann's Magic Rose Cubes hung on a trellis constructed of origami PHZ units (pentagon-hexagon-zig zag) units designed by Tom Hull. Window art by Richard Alexander and Ashley Woodward at Origamido Studio.

PAPER SELECTION

By Michael LaFosse and Richard Alexander

Every origami artist often struggles to find the "perfect" paper for a given model. Even at the Origamido Studio, where we have the capability to make paper by hand, considerable trial, error, and testing goes on before we are satisfied with the paper we produce for a given project. However, many origami artists are usually happy to just find paper that handles the required folds well—"suitable," if not "perfect" paper. It may not be exactly what is desired, but it will do. Often an origami artist will find success working with a particular type of paper, whether it is tissue-foil, Elephant Hide™, or watercolor paper, and then stay within the technical boundaries of that particular paper. This is like a painter making do with only one or two kinds of brushes.

In our previous book, *Japanese Paper Crafting* (Tuttle Publishing), we presented a variety of techniques for making your own paper, and more practically, techniques for back-coating, stiffening, and otherwise making previously unsuitable papers suitable for your origami art. We will review some of the most useful techniques here, including preparing methyl cellulose, an archival bonding agent and stiffener. When methyl cellulose is used to bond two sheets of thinner or softer papers together, the composite can be more easily wet-folded. It is a great way to make "duo," or two-colored papers for models such as the Birdwing Butterfly that benefit from contrasting colors.

Too few origami artists consider coloring their papers. Acrylic paints provide the artist an opportunity to become familiar with a particular type of folding stock, for instance, watercolor paper, and then modify its look with more appropriate shades of color. Rarely, but increasingly, some origami art is painted or colored after the model is folded, but this can be tricky, since the added water can loosen the crispness of the folds. Some artists have used colored pencil and other mixtures of colorants to great success.

Many folders work through a variety of media in a predictable sequence as they develop their skills as origami artists. Often they begin by folding inexpensive "kami," slang for the readily available, 6 or 10-inch square origami paper colored only on one side, popularized for more than a century for elementary school use. As the models become more involved, and 10-inch kami becomes insufficient, the folder with inter-mediate skills often begins to use spray adhesive to back thinner tissue with aluminum foil. Thicker substitutes include florists' foil and some gift-wrapping papers. Eventually, these artists realize the volatile nature of the wood-pulp tissues and spray glues used in those works, and graduate to archivally-pigmented, handmade papers from strong, longer plant fibers.

There are many inexpensive papers on the market from Southeast Asia that are made by machine, and are not considered colorfast. The origami artist needs to be cautious with these, or expect to augment the color on the paper's surface with acrylic paints before folding a piece of origami artwork. Many of these papers will also require back-coating before folding, and so bonding with a high quality kozo, using methyl cellulose, can make the acrylic-enhanced, decorative papers quite suitable.

Facing page: Hand-crumpled Momigami, natural, dyed and gilded.

Should you decide to prepare and produce your own handmade paper for an origami art project, we can refer you not only to the *Japanese Paper Crafting* title, but also our previous book, *Advanced Origami* (also by Tuttle Publishing), and some our video lessons, such as *Origami Sea Turtle & Koi*, *Origami Penguin & Squirrel*, or the *LaFosse Origami Frog* on DVD, available through the www.origamido.com website. There are also several other good resources for hand papermakers, and while they are not typically tuned into the needs of origami artists, the Internet is a great way to follow their offerings.

Should you decide to explore the higher quality offerings at your local paper or arts supply stores, here are a few types of papers you should consider for your art:

NATURAL WASHI

This type of paper is unbleached or non-dyed Japanese paper from fibers of mitsumata, kozo, or gampi (different plants specifically cultivated in Japan for their fiber). Washi may also contain various blends of these fibers. Natural washi is a good choice for the origami artist, since the absence of color allows you to add only the pigments that you want in your model. You can control the use of colorants that you know to be archival. These natural washi papers are available in varying thicknesses and can be made quite suitable for origami art with a little effort.

Below: Natural washi.

Gampi

Thin gampi is fantastic for origami insects because it is thin, strong, crisp, and glossy.

Mitsumata

This fiber is strong, and often slightly toothier (with a rougher surface) than gampi. It is a good, all-purpose folding paper you should keep on hand for a variety of folding uses.

Kozo

The paper mulberry's supple bast fibers are from a tree the Japanese call kozo, which is plentiful and less expensive than mitsumata or gampi. Kozo has been more widely cultivated, so it is easiest to find, and is available in a great variety of thicknesses.

Natural Blends

It is hard to tell which fibers are in many of the available blends. The inexpensive blends might include some wood pulp. More expensive papers may include some abaca, a strong fiber from a plant in the banana family. Much of the abaca is grown in the Philippines, and is commonly used for teabags.

Other countries in Asia also now produce washi-like papers from a wide variety of similar plants, but often call their papers by different names. For example, Hanji is handmade Korean paper. Thailand and India have tremendous selections of natural papers, as well as dyed papers.

Above left: Dyed washi.

Above right: Unryu.

DYED WASHI

Dye colors are often organic molecules, and may be quite fugitive (or prone to fading) when compared to ground mineral pigments. These inexpensive dyed papers may be wonderful for experimenting, and are certainly suitable for origami art used in one-time party celebrations. Since they are generally not fade resistant, be sure to display these works away from bright sunlight.

Momigami

Hand-crumpled momigami has a wonderfully wrinkled texture, and is often suitable for folding renditions of origami animals with heavily textured skin, like the elephant and the Rhinoceros. The wrinkles also expose the ends of the fibers, and so momigami can also be used to fold models of creatures with hair or fur.

Unryu

Unryu papers are characterized by wispy, underbeaten, cloud-like fibers. Often unryu papers are available as extremely thin sheets, but these may also contain holes and visible clumps of unbeaten fibers that interfere with precision folding.

Rag Bond

These fine papers are actually made from beating recycled rags. They vary in content from about 20% to 100% cotton or linen rags. This paper is strong but flexible, and is an excellent choice for wet-folding. It can be difficult to find large sheets of rag bond. The lighter weights are excellent for origami airplanes, such as the F-14 Tomcat Fighter Jet design in this book.

Abaca Tissue

Abaca tissue is available from specialty sources that supply museums and libraries with archival book conservation materials, and is available in rolls or sheets. This strong, machine made tissue should be back-coated, and can also be colored before folding. It is excellent for complex and super-complex origami masterworks.

WATERCOLOR PAPERS

Watercolor papers are readily available in any art supply store. For origami, choose from the thinnest weights, since these papers are heavily sized, or infused with chemical stiffener, such as gelatine. Squares from roll stock and large sheets of watercolor paper can be difficult to work with: they resist folding until moistened; they often require two people to handle; sometimes become too floppy during the folding process, and pucker as they dry. Despite these problems, rolled watercolor papers do produce durable, large, elegant wet-folded pieces. Most of the thinner watercolor

Below left: Rag Bond.
Below right: Abaca Tissue.

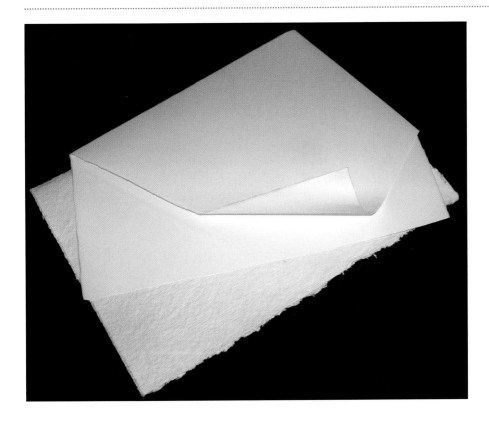

Watercolor Papers.

papers are suitable for simple to intermediate models, due to their relative thickness. Of course, they are designed to take color, and also glue or paste. Their bright white finish makes watercolor papers a favorite for our commercial art, when we need to create large, sculptural, often multi-piece origami-esque constructions.

COLORED ART PAPERS

Art papers (also called artists' papers) come in many different colors, brands, finishes, and weights or thicknesses.

The thinner papers are best for more complex origami creations, but these papers tend to tear easily, due to the high content of short fibers of wood pulp. Formulated to be quite fade resistant, quality varies from color to color and from one manufacturer to another. These sheets are nearly all available as large rectangles, so it is best to cut your paper square, then test a remnant scrap, wet-folding it to see if and how the colors may bleed onto your table, come off on your hands, how much punishment the paper will take, and so forth. Art papers, such as Strathmore Artist Papers™, Canson® and Canford™ brands tend to fade less than some others. Canford™ is a heavier, stiffer, smoother art paper best used for large commercial window displays of origami-esque construction. Canson® Mi Teintes® is somewhat thinner, and so can be used effectively for more complex origami models.

ELEPHANT HIDE™ AND WYNDSTONE™

This is a hard, smooth, almost plastic-like art paper quite popular with origami artists due to its surface texture, strength and shapability. It is heavily sized, but the colors do fade when exposed to sunlight, so display these artworks carefully. Wyndstone™ is a similar material, also quite popular with origami artists because of its surface textures and wet-folding possibilities.

Above left: Colored art papers.

Above right: Elephant Hide™.

OTHER MATERIALS

Inexpensive, hamburger patty papers are sold through restaurant suppliers, and are often perfectly square, wood pulp, bleached white, and/or translucent from wax or polymer coating. Patty papers are especially suitable to class projects involving thousands of models, such as garlands of cranes. They have also been successfully used by teachers to illustrate concepts in Plane Geometry, when the translucent sheets are folded on an overhead projector.

MAKING YOUR OWN PAPER

With so many wonderful, wet-foldable papers available to you at a reasonable price, why would you want to make your own paper? There are several reasons. Most likely, the color, texture, size, or thickness of commercially available paper is not quite right for your project. Perhaps you may not be sure about the quality of the fibers or pigments, and need to know for sure that the color, indeed the paper itself will last. As an artist, you may insist upon complete control over the look of your final work, and recognize that handmade paper will add an element of distinction, enhancing the experience of each viewer.

That said; why not make your own paper for all of your works?

Making your own paper does take some time and effort, but it is also fun. We have described Eastern and Western methods in our last hardcover book, *Japanese Paper Crafting* (Tuttle Publishing). In our book, *Advanced Origami* (Tuttle Publishing) we have also described the papermaking process that we use most often in the workshops we hold at the Origamido Studio. This section will briefly describe the method we have used at home to produce a small number of sheets of handmade paper suitable for wet-folding some of the projects in this book. Of course, the suitability of the handmade paper will depend upon your choice of materials, equipment, techniques, and skill. At first, you may not be able to make uniform sheets that are also thin enough for some of the more complex models. In any event, trying to make your own paper will give you a valuable understanding of the papermaking process, and educate you about how choices in the process affect the qualities of papers made by others. (Read through this entire section before you try this, if you are inclined to replicate this process at home.)

Fiber Selection

There are several suppliers listed on the Internet that can send you a bucket of pre-beaten pulp containing the fibers of your choice. We recommend you begin by using abaca, a strong fiber from the banana family. Kozo, mitsumata, gampi, cotton, hemp, and flax are also suitable fibers, and we often blend them to produce papers with different characteristics. When you purchase a 5-gallon bucket of beaten pulp, what have they done that you do not have to do? Somebody has grown, selected, and harvested the plants, stripped the bast fibers, boiled off the soft tissue with alkali, rinsed the fiber and removed bark impurities, and then mechanically splayed the fibers of cellulose.

If they have done all this, when you order a bucket of beaten pulp, have you really made your own paper? YES! You have paid for properly selected and pre-processed, high quality fibers, as well as paying for the LACK of chlorine, sulfur and short fiber, cheaper wood pulp. You will probably have about 2 pounds (dry weight) in the bucket of wet, beaten fiber. That's enough for 200 sheets of paper, so work with friends.

Coloring

Should you decide to color your pulp before forming the sheets, prepare to handle, weigh, and mix chemicals. In the Paper Preparation section, we offered a simpler alternative technique, namely, applying acrylic color to the natural or white sheet when it is dry. The same company you ordered your pre-beaten pulp from, also sells a chemical called "retention agent" and various archival pigments. The retention agent is a polymer that imparts an opposite charge to the bonding sites on the cellulose molecule. Different coloring systems use different cationic or anionic polymers to make your paper colorfast. Do not mix components made by different manufacturers. Stay with the recommended components of the chosen coloring system!

Au Naturel?

One of our hand papermaking expert friends took a trip to the Southwest US one summer, collecting colorful earth in plastic bags at several different locations. He made the most amazing palette of archival, earth-toned papers we have ever seen. If you experiment with earth pigments, be sure to grind them to fine powder, and conscientiously use a dust mask! Be sure you are not introducing organic carbon, or humus to your paper, since these materials are not chemically stabile, and will cause your paper to decompose with considerable odor.

Sheet Forming

Here's the fun part. You will need a vat, a paper maker's framed screen and deckle frame. You can even make the framed screen from inexpensive components purchased at your local arts and crafts store. You can purchase an inexpensive polyethylene vat, approximately 22 x 34, and 8.5 inches deep, designed for mixing concrete, at your local home improvement or hardware store.

If you do not have a screen yet, measure your vat before you buy or make your screen. You need at least four or five inches of free space between your screen frame, and the back side of the tub. If your tub is 22 inches wide, you can easily scoop a sheet of pulp on a screen that will produce a piece of paper 16 x 20 inches. (By holding the frame on the shorter ends.) Find a pair of suitably sized, old wooden picture frames, stretch some window screen tightly over one, stapling it to the back of the first frame.

With about five or six inches of water in the vat, dilute the pulp in the water and disperse it with your hands, so that there is enough in suspension to just obscure a dime on the bottom of the tub. A good starting point is to add 5% of your beaten pulp to the vat. (After you attempt to make a sheet, you will be able to adjust the pulp concentration accordingly.)

Hold the second, open frame (deckle) firmly on top of the flat side of the screen as you dip it into the vat of pulp. Now that you have scooped pulp onto the screen, level and raise the deckle frame and screen until the water drains away. Remove the open frame (deckle), and see how evenly the pulp appears on the screen. Not even? Throw it back by flipping the screen over, gently contacting the wet pulp back onto the surface of the slurry in the tub. Re-disperse the pulp with your hands before trying again.

Couching

That's French for "putting it to bed." When you have an even layer of pulp on the screen, you need to get it off. Some ancient hand paper making methods involve placing the screen with the wet pulp in the sun, then peeling the sheet of paper off the screen when it is dry. You probably want to make another sheet, so transfer the wet pulp onto a slightly larger wet layer of felt supported on a slightly larger board (1/2-inch plywood is fine), inverting the screen onto the wet felt, then blotting the back of the screen with another absorbent, wrung-out cloth or sponge, before you carefully lift the screen away. If the pulp stays behind, you have successfully "couched" it! Cover it with another wet felt, and repeat the process, forming a stack or "post."

After you are through making paper, form a funnel from another piece of window screen, and strain the pulp before disposing the water, to prevent your plugging the drain pipes. The pulp should keep for about a week.

Pressing

Adding pressure at this point does several things, but essentially, it makes stronger, more uniform sheets by removing the majority of the water. Take the stack of wet pulp and wet felts outside, add another piece of plywood to the top, and then pile on the weight. Water will come out. Leave the pressure on for at least 20 minutes.

Drying

After removing most of the water, carefully peel the felt off the pulp layer, then pinch and pull the pulp at the corner to carefully remove it from the felt beneath. If you made only a few sheets, apply the moist mat of paper to a clean windowpane, using a clean, soft, wide, dry brush. The moisture will keep it in place. As the paper dries, it usually starts to come away from the glass.

If you made several sheets, separate each wet layer of pulp between a pair of slightly larger blotters. Separate each set between corrugated cardboard, making sure the corrugations all run in the same direction. Use a plastic garbage bag and some packing tape to direct air from a box fan through the corrugations. Add some weight to the stack to keep the cardboards from curling as they absorb water from the paper. Usually adequate drying takes place overnight.

Larger Sheets

You can make larger sheets without making a larger screen frame. As you apply the wet, pressed pulp to a windowpane, you can overlap the sheets slightly, and then gently tap the area of overlap until the two sheets become joined. We have carefully smoothed these seams with a paint roller, sponge, and several other tools. The size of your paper is limited only by the size of the windowpane you decide to use.

Larger Duo Sheets

Without taking the first paper off the window, go ahead and brush on a coating of methyl cellulose. (See Preparing Paste.) Apply a second layer of different colored, pressed pulp, making sure the seams are staggered, and do not coincide with the seams on the first sheet. See also Making Larger Sheets in the next chapter.

Four-sheet strip with joined lap seams.

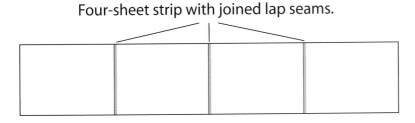

Forty-sheet back-coated assembly.

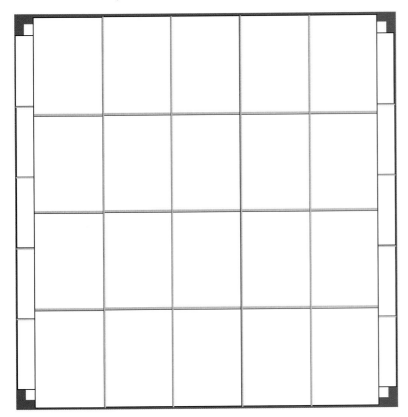

Overlapped, staggered, and layered sheets.

TECHNIQUES

By Michael LaFosse

By mastering a few useful techniques, you can make otherwise unsuitable papers useful for folding. This chapter shows how to prepare and use archival paste to stiffen too-soft papers, laminate sheets together, make "duo-color" papers, and large sheets for complex, and super-complex origami art.

PREPARING PASTE

There are two basic forms of methyl cellulose paste: Methyl Cellulose (MC), and Sodium Carboxy Methyl Cellulose (CMC). Either will work. However, always use premium grades: they are purer and archival. Methyl cellulose products can be purchased from art supply stores, and from bookbinding and papermaking supply houses. Several suppliers are listed at the back of this book. Some products must be made up using room temperature water, while others must first be dissolved in a small quantity of boiling water and then finished with ice water. Read the directions on the package to know which method to use.

Methyl cellulose is sold as a white powder. You will mix it with water to the desired consistency. Start with a ratio of one part powder to eight parts water. This will work for most applications. It is best to prepare methyl cellulose paste the day before you will use it. Letting it stand overnight maximizes the uptake of water by the solids and allows entrained air bubbles to escape. Your patience will be rewarded with a smoother paste that is easier to work with. The prepared paste is easy to store and keeps well for a long time.

Store the paste in a clean container with a tight-fitting lid. The paste will become spoiled if contaminates are introduced, so be sure to always remove paste from the storage container using clean utensils. Do not return unused paste to the main storage container as brushes and your hands could have contaminated the working supply. Keep refrigerated in hot and humid climates or if you have indoor problems with mold.

Facing page: Compound origami plant, in handmade Origamido™ paper. Each element is from a single square. The elements are assembled on paper-covered wire. Prepared for the FLorigami Exhibit, Morikami Museum, Delray Beach, FL, 2005.

Below: Basic materials for preparing papers for back-coating and wet-folding.

Mixing Methyl Cellulose with Water

Materials list: Mixing bowl, whisk, water, methyl cellulose powder, clean container, volumetric measuring tools, clean salt or spice shaker (optional).

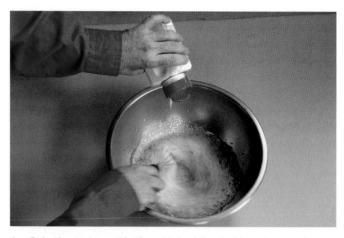

1. Stir the water with the whisk while shaking the powder lightly upon the surface. Stir and sprinkle until all of the powder has been added to the water.

2. Let this mixture sit for an hour or so; then stir out any remaining lumps. Transfer to a clean storage container and let sit overnight.

3. Clear and clean MC paste, ready to use!

Blender Method

1. To a half full pitcher of water, set the mixer on low and gradually sprinkle in the powder.

2. Transfer to a clean storage container. The air bubbles will disappear when you let the mixture stand overnight.

BACK-COATING

Many papers must be properly prepared before they can be used for wet-folding origami projects. This is especially true for many Asian papers, which are soft and cloth-like. Wet-folding relies upon the glue-like substance that is inherent in most Western-style papers and which makes such papers hard and stiff. This material is called *size*, and it may be made from a natural starch, or protein, such as animal derived gelatin; but it may also be synthetic. Whatever the source, this glue is invested in or applied to the surface of the paper, making it able to support printing and writing inks without bleeding, and making the paper tough and durable against the abrading actions of pens and printing machines.

Papers treated with size are ready to use, off the shelf, for wet-folding. However, there are many un-sized papers, which have other desirable properties for origami projects, which can only be used after a size has been applied somehow. One method is to back-coat: two or more sheets are pasted together, containing the size between them. The following method can be used for all kinds of papers, and it is useful for the stiffening of fabrics, too.

Materials: Methyl cellulose paste (The powder in the bag, see Preparing Paste in the Techniques Section) a wet brush (in the bowl of paste), a dry brush (wide, with short bristles), water in a spray bottle.

1. One sheet of paper is first trimmed to be one inch shorter in each dimension. Lightly spray water over both sides of both sheets of paper. The papers will drink up this water, expanding somewhat and mitigating the problem of a dry paper pulling water out of the paste. As wet paste is applied, dry paper will cockle and distort, and the paste will be difficult to apply smoothly.

2. Brush the paste evenly over the entire larger sheet.

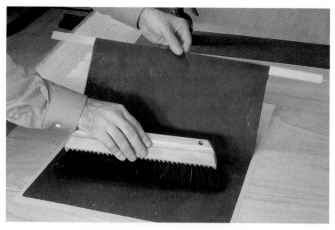

3. Lay the smaller sheet on top of the paste layer. A wooden dowel is helpful with larger sheets. Apply pressure smoothly with a dry brush, brushing out air bubbles as you go along.

4. Apply extra paste around the edges of the larger sheet.

5. Place a narrow strip of dry paper across the exposed paste, extending into the dry area and beyond the paper's edge. This will serve as a gateway through the paste and aid in removal of the sheet from the drying surface.

6. Turn the sheet over and brush it against a wooden board or other stiff, wide surface, such as a counter top or sheet of glass. Allow to dry overnight.

7. Remove the dry paper using a knife or a letter opener. Begin by sliding the blade of the tool under the paper through the gateway. Run the blade around the perimeter until it releases from the surface. Remnant scraps of paper and glue can be soaked off.

8. The back-coated sheet is ready to trim and wet-fold.

ACRYLIC PAINTS AND COLORANTS

There are many advantages to using acrylic paints and colorants to prepare the paper for your origami art. Acrylics can be purchased in tubes of concentrated pigments, or in jars or bottles already diluted for use. Before the acrylic polymers cross-link in the drying process, they can be thinned with water or acrylic medium to create lighter washes.

Tube acrylics tend to be more economical, since they require less space on the shelf, and can be thinned with water or acrylic thinner for lighter washes. Thinning the acrylics with acrylic polymer (binder or flow medium) helps extend the drying time, while preserving the brush flow characteristics, film strength and color evenness.

Some acrylics contain iridescent luster pigments, usually from ground mica, a mineral often used in cosmetics. The luster pigments make excellent paper for origami butterflies, and for shiny or wet animals. We often incorporate luster pigments in hand-made paper for the Grackle, Alligator, and Cormorant. We urge you to experiment with the interference luster pigments. These are usually powders of ground mica, a naturally occurring mineral, processed to a specific size that produces sparkling color due to the particle's interaction with light of only the desired wavelengths. We have best success adding luster to darker base papers, such as black or dark purple. Be sure to choose colors that are safe to work with, listed as Non Toxic, and rated high for colorfastness. Keep in mind how these materials actually work: Often mixing these lustrous paints will destroy the beauty of the finish, since their luster depends upon the uniform presence of a specific particle size, in order to capture and reflect specific wavelengths of light. Mixing these particle sizes muddies the reflection.

Acrylic paints for the fine artist come in many different formulations. We suggest trying some formulated for airbrush application. These tend to flow well, even when applied by brush. If you have the equipment, the paper can be coated with an airbrush spray. Before any application of acrylics, adjust the moisture in the paper so it will not pucker wildly. We use a simple atomizer or plant mister to condition the paper to take water-based acrylic paints.

Acrylic paints also come in spray cans. These are often formulated for exterior use, and produce a tough, hard-looking finish. They dry quickly, but the coated papers can be difficult to fold. When choosing any chemical, always look for the least toxic option. Many artists' materials will bear a non-toxic designation, but there are still plenty of coatings that are dangerous to handle and dispose of. Use only as directed, with plenty of ventilation. Remember that when you fold these colored papers, your hands will be contacting the finish, so chemical safety is important. Wash your hands thoroughly, both before and after handling the coated papers.

MAKING LARGE SHEETS

It is sometimes desirable to make very large origami models. Some origami designs produce models that are a tiny fraction of the area of a sheet of paper. In either case it is necessary to procure sheets of paper in excess of a meter square. Other than cutting squares from large rolls of cheap paper, there is only one practical option and that is to build up large sheets from smaller ones. The following method combines tiling multiple sheets with back-coating, producing a strong sheet that is perfect for wet-folding. This method will allow you to prepare paper for the folding of the American Alligator, featured in this book.

Materials: 40 Sheets of washi; Polyvinyl Acetate (PVA) glue; methyl cellulose or starch paste. A small flat brush to apply the PVA glue and a wide soft brush for the paste.

1. Apply PVA glue along one of the narrow edges of a sheet of washi. The glue line should not be wider than $1/2$ inch.

2. Overlap this glue edge on the short edge of another sheet. Attach a total of four sheets in a row. Build up four more strips in this manner. Let dry completely.

3. Once the five strips are dry and the glue bonds are solid, run a line of glue along the long edge of one strip.

4. Overlap the glue edge of the first strip onto the long edge of one of the other strips. Continue in this manner until all of the strips are joined into one large sheet. Let dry completely.

5. Make your second sheet in the same manner using the other twenty sheets. You can then paste the two sheets together, following the back-coating method covered earlier in this chapter. Refer to the diagram on page 39. Trim square after drying. If color is desired it is best to paint each separate sheet before assembly, since the paint will take up differently where the PVA has been applied. Let the paint dry completely before commencing to glue-up.

Back-coating large sheets can be problematic since the area of the work surface must be at least as large as the final sheet. A plastic drop cloth placed on the floor will work in place of a suitable work table. At the Origamido Studio we made excellent use of a 6-foot by 6-foot safety glass panel, which was supported by two large folding tables. The glass was smooth and flat, and easy to clean. For best results, the paper must be dried while restrained around the edges. A wooden frame of two-by-fours can be quickly fabricated to the proper size and the edges of the paper can be attached to the frame with glue or a staple gun. Use stainless steel staples.

BUILDING FLOWERS AND PLANTS

Modular flowers and compound-origami plants are an area of specialty that has a history all its own. Many origami enthusiasts have traditionally shunned the option to build up models from multiple sheets, and, dare I say the words "Use Glue!" However, several notable origami masters are pioneers in this field: Akira Yoshizawa, Yoshihide Momotani and Dr. James Sakoda. Their developments in this area are legendary and inspiring. Each of these masters have carefully studied the living plants and have contributed style and methods all their own. There is still a lot of work left to be done in this field. I hope that these few simple lessons will inspire you.

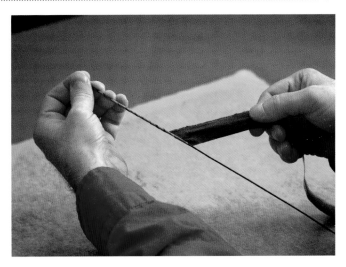

Materials: Florist wire of varying thicknesses; paste or white glue; small brush to apply the paste; strips of paper to cover the wire; origami blossoms and leaves. The leaves already have wires included, as recommended in the folding method.

1. Apply paste to one side of a narrow strip of paper. Select a heavy gauge of wire and, beginning at the top, wrap the strip in a winding spiral all the way to the bottom. If you run out of paper before reaching the bottom, apply a new strip and continue on until the wire is completely covered. I am using paper colored differently on both sides to emphasize the spiral pattern for this demonstration. This layer is the "base layer" and is only meant to cover the bare wire with a base for the other appliances to come. Let the stem dry completely.

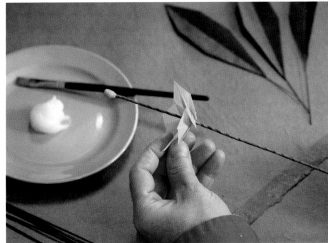

2. Use the brush to apply a little paste to the inside center of the flower blossom.

3. Use paste and paper to build a small ball-shaped tip on the top end of the wire stem. Pass the bottom end of the stem through the center hole of the blossom. Press the paste and paper ball to the inside base of the blossom, taking care not to dislodge the wire. This paper center could just as easily be an origami element or additional, smaller blossoms, making a more complex design. Let dry completely.

4. Start a new strip of pasted paper under the base of the blossom and wind down to the point where you wish to attach your first leaf. Place the wire of the leaf against the stem and wind the pasted paper over it. Notice that the top edge of the paper strip is ragged. This effect was achieved by tearing the paper, not cutting it with a tool. The ragged edge will blend in softly against the outside of the stem, making the seams less visible. Continue until all leaves are attached. You can use different sizes of leaves. You can vary the shades of green, lighter for the younger ones and darker for the mature ones. So many possibilities!

BASIC FOLDS

Here's a quick review of the basic folds with which you should be familiar.

Edge to Crease

Most folds are created by aligning edges or points, or by placing an edge on a crease, then decreasing the bend until the two planes are flat. The beginner will often use visual signals to decide when the edge lines up. More advanced folders will align edges by feeling for the alignment. As you look carefully before placing the crease, be sure to bend your head over the alignment so that you can look straight across the two edges of paper, perpendicular to the table. A folder who does this realizes that every sheet of paper has a thickness. Understanding and accounting for that third dimension is helpful when planning to eliminate gaps after reversing certain creases. Wet-folders using thicker papers tend to learn this quickly.

Inside Reverse Fold

When you pull a point between the outer layers of paper, you often turn a portion of a mountain fold into a valley fold. This maneuver is called the inside reverse fold.

Outside Reverse Fold

When you pull paper back over itself to enclose the other two layers of paper, you also turn the tip of the paper over, showing the other side. This maneuver is called the outside reverse fold.

Rabbit Ear

When you pull in paper from two directions and are left with excess that sticks up in the middle, the maneuver is called a rabbit ear.

Squash Fold

When you raise a multilayered flap perpendicular to the table and any remaining paper, open the layers of the raised portion, and then press the center mountain fold flat to the table, this is called a squash fold.

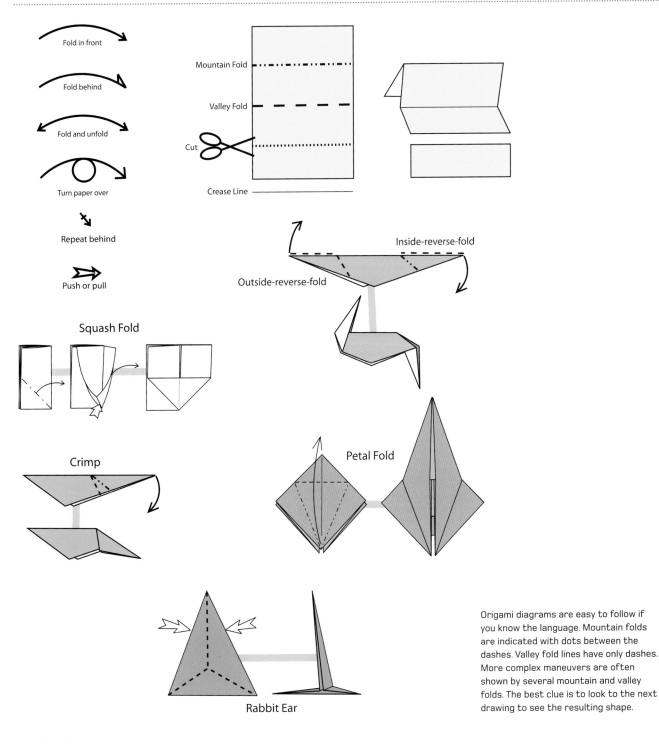

Fold in front

Fold behind

Fold and unfold

Turn paper over

Repeat behind

Push or pull

Mountain Fold

Valley Fold

Cut

Crease Line

Squash Fold

Outside-reverse-fold

Inside-reverse-fold

Crimp

Petal Fold

Rabbit Ear

Origami diagrams are easy to follow if you know the language. Mountain folds are indicated with dots between the dashes. Valley fold lines have only dashes. More complex maneuvers are often shown by several mountain and valley folds. The best clue is to look to the next drawing to see the resulting shape.

Petal Fold

When you pull a point across the other layers of paper, lengthening the form by bringing in paper from the sides to cover the top, you are making a petal fold.

Sink

When you reverse the mountains and valleys that form a point or peak, in order to create an indented form, this maneuver is called a sink.

Crimp

When you grasp a folded piece of paper and insert a symmetrical, mirror-image pair of mountain and valley folds on either side of the central mountain fold, the central mountain fold changes direction due to a maneuver called a crimp.

The advanced folding techniques used for the projects in this book include curved folds and wet-folding. These techniques do take time to master, but they are essential for creating complex models.

WET-FOLDING

Wet-folding is a fairly recent technique in the history of origami. It is widely agreed that this method was pioneered and popularized by the great master, Akira Yoshizawa. Master Yoshizawa was a keen student of the papers of Japan, their preparations and applications, and he was a trained and skilled calligrapher. Among the many things that a Japanese calligrapher would learn would be the selection of fine papers and their preparation for mounting and display. This would include the technique that we call "back-coating" and it involves the pasting of two or more sheets of paper together to stiffen and support the art in preparation for mounting as a hanging scroll. The traditional techniques are elaborate and require a great deal of study and experience. Otherwise the mount will not well survive the passing of time and the seasonal changes of climate.

Master Yoshizawa adapted these traditional techniques to stiffen and otherwise prepare fine Japanese papers for folding. These papers, stiffened with paste, yield most gracefully to the folder's hands when lightly moistened with water. The water temporarily softens the paste layer and the paper can be folded, softly or firmly and with geometric precision or with lyrical curves. When dry the paper is quite rigid, and so the folded sculpture resists unfolding or becoming misshapen. Master Yoshizawa's vision for his work and his original style were born of and made possible by the wet-folding technique: it is a style that is well suited to origami which represents living subjects; as gesture and movement can be implied as well as in any other art form. By now many in the origami community have seen wet-folded sculptures, and many have tried this technique or have made it their chosen style. Indeed, it is my chosen style, and most of the models in this book are best made this way. The following demonstration will aid those new to wet-folding and will be a guide to the methods best used throughout this book.

Applying Water

There are many ways to apply water to your paper. By far the best method is to use a fine mist from a spray bottle. Have handy a wide, soft brush, or a moistened cloth towel or sponge to aid in spreading the water across the sheet. You should hold the spray bottle some distance from the surface of the paper and you must pump the trigger firmly to get the finest spray. Distance and a fine spray are essential because you need to moisten the paper lightly and evenly. Move the spray bottle as you pump and be sure to get the edges and corners evenly covered.

Notice here that the paper has curled. It has curled parallel to the direction of the grain in the paper. If the paper has little to no grain, as some handmade papers do, the paper will bubble and cockle randomly. In order to remove the curl you must spray the back side of the paper, too. The reason for the curl is that the side that soaked in the water first has expanded. Effectively, this side is now wider than the other side. Adding water to the back will correct this disparity and the sheet will relax flat again.

A properly moistened sheet is flat and will not look wet. Feel the paper, it should feel cool to the touch and it should be pliant like a piece of leather. The paper must never be soggy, limp or mushy. Too much water and you will likely damage your sheet when you try to fold it. Better let it dry out somewhat before you start in.

Because your sheet has expanded mostly parallel to the grain, your square will no longer be equilateral. The more water you add, the greater the expansion. This is another reason to avoid adding too much water, especially at the beginning. Some people like to wet the paper and cut it square after. You should experiment to see which school of thought you prefer.

Sharp Creases

Sharp creases are best made with the back of the thumbnail. This will burnish the folded edge neatly, without leaving any scars. The side edge of your thumbnail, especially if ragged, will leave scars.

You can use a folding tool, such as a bone folder or the bottom bowl of a metal spoon.

Curved Creases

Curved and softer creases are made with the thumb and fingertips. You can make multiple, soft pinches, or you can use a gliding, smooth stroke, like free-drawing with a pencil.

The best results are achieved in the air, away from the surface of the table.

Adding Methyl Cellulose While Folding

We have described using methyl cellulose paste to bond two or more sheets of paper together (see Back Coating). We also use methyl cellulose to moisten specific areas of a model as we complete the folding process through the final shaping phase. Here are a few hints and tips that you might find helpful.

- We sometimes add methyl cellulose at the final stages to impart a size, or stiffener to the narrow appendages, such as to legs or antennae, restraining those in exactly the desired position as they dry fully. Think of it as a type of hair styling gel, many of which contain methyl cellulose!

- The methyl cellulose paste is an ideal material to use to re-wet only a specific area of the model. Use a small brush or other applicator to apply the paste to only that area, to provide more working time than you could achieve using water alone. It allows the artist to concentrate more on the art, and not as much on the technical requirements of constantly having to apply mists of water here or there as the model dries unevenly during the folding process. As with using water, we leave our model in a plastic bag when we need to leave the project for a prolonged period of time, or even if we want the moisture to become more uniformly distributed throughout the model.

- We also use the methyl cellulose to smooth areas of the model that may have become fuzzy, or abraded. It acts as a surface finish when you smooth it with your finger or brush. Softer, Asian papers are easily abraded, and benefit most from this repair technique.

Use of Restraints While Drying

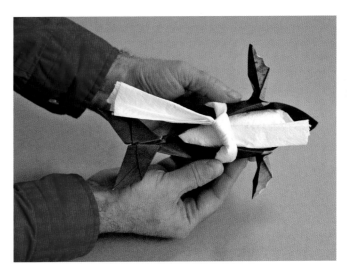

Because wet-folded models are often three-dimensional, you will want to engineer supports and restraints for them while they dry. This is especially true with larger sculptures. You should never use hard-edged devices, such as paper clips and clamps, directly against the surface of the paper. You should instead supply some kind of cushioning material between the clip and the paper to prevent embossing and scarring.

Soft chord, strips of cloth or paper can be used to tie selected areas closed. It is sometimes desirable to stuff some crumpled paper towel inside large cavities to keep them from collapsing.

PREPARING ORIGAMI FOR DISPLAY

By Richard Alexander

MOUNTING

Often origami art is created for the pleasure of the creator, with no thought about how the object will be appreciated by anybody else. Michael's Happy, Good-Luck Bats have been popular commissions for weddings, anniversaries and house-warming parties. We developed a method of adding an attachment strap to the back of each bat, that can be glued onto the background paper within the shadowbox.

Most often a special wire mount is formed from stainless steel or brass wire, or perhaps acrylic or brass rod stock for heavier origami models. The wires or rods usually insert into internal, folded pockets—sometimes designed into the folding sequence—that enable the work to be properly positioned and supported without having to glue or affix any other attachments. Usually the wire or rod is inserted into a drilled hole at the base, which must be heavy enough to prevent the display from tipping. We have used several types of wood for bases, including driftwood, burl, birdseye maple blocks, and velvet-covered beveled pine.

We have constructed pedestals from driftwood posts, carpet-covered Foamcore™ and wooden boxes. Pedestal tops, or slabs, should complement the origami art, and we have had fun selecting square tiles, marble, granite, and decorative wood before designing the base to support the slab. When another business in our building vacated their offices, they left behind a series of laminated shelves with trimmed edges that we covered in our hand-made paper. Most of the wall mounts and table mounts used in the FLorigami show were reclaimed shelf slabs that we covered in hand-made paper from the same Everglades palette.

Casual mounts

My mother enjoys displaying Michael's origami butterflies. When we published the book describing his butterfly design system, we had a large display (portable show booth Expand-a-Wall) with dozens of butterflies folded from our hand-made papers mounted on Velcro™ dots. Customers enjoyed being able to mix and match their favorite butterflies onto their favorite handmade background papers in different shadow box frames. The removable butterflies made it quite easy to change butterflies with the season, or whenever the color scheme in a room may need updating. Joyce Saler has popularized mounting origami on clothing, backpacks, curtains, and table settings. Magnetic disks provide a completely removable and non-destructive method of wearing and sharing origami with others.

Facing page: Alexander Aztec Swallowtails on Purple Munich Orchid, by Michael G. LaFosse & Richard L. Alexander, 2007. Compound origami composition of handmade Origamido™ papers.

FRAMING

Origami art is always a framing challenge. The fact is that most people have more wall space than room for works on pedestals, consequently, if any origami is on display, it is probably in a wall mount.

Years ago, almost every home had curio cabinets. My grandmother had a lit, free-standing corner unit with bowed glass where she kept her finest hand-painted china. These cabinets would be great for some origami models. We often design origami models to be framed in commercially available deep shadow box frames. Art supply chain stores carry a fine selection of basic shadow box frames, which can be spiced up by adding more framing around the perimeter.

Many of Michael's custom works defy anything except custom framing, and to keep costs down, we have often married multiple frames together to make inexpensive, deep frames. Standard frames often allow you to select pre-cut mats.

A custom framing job can easily cost more than the origami art. Hopefully, as people come to appreciate the unique qualities of origami art, the value will increase and people will entertain custom enclosures.

Several of the art supply chains also offer inexpensive doll cases and sport memorabilia cases suitable for displaying origami art. We have had custom plastics firms create dozens of acrylic bonnets for various shows, but these are easily scuffed in transit, and require frequent dusting, especially when the art is properly lit.

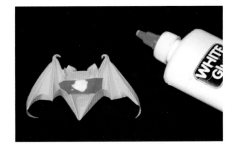

Facing page: Kangaroo and Joey, by Michael LaFosse, poised on a velvet covered display block designed by Alexander; formed by slitting the corners of beveled pine blocks, then pulling the velvet into the saw kerf.

Above: Adding an attachment strap to the back of each piece, that can in turn be glued onto the background paper.

Left: Oblique view of deep framed origami abstract Portrait of a Friend by Michael G. LaFosse.

Above: Detail showing the joining of two standard frames to form a deeper shadow box suitable for 3D origami display.

Top: Some displays have too many objects.

Above: Some crowded displays work because of some underlying theme.

DESIGNING THE DISPLAY AREA

The display area for showing origami works must be uncluttered. This is particularly difficult for the origami artist, who often keeps every previous version and step fold for reference. Even at origami conventions, artists eager to show a large quantity of work will often make the mistake of cluttering their exhibits.

The viewer needs time and space to absorb the beauty of an exquisite piece of origami art. The initial presence of a piece may draw the viewer from across the room by its shape, subject matter or color. When the viewer gets closer, details such as folding qualities—regularity, ratios, proportions, angles, crispness, and even the texture of the paper—keep the viewer engaged. Some origami is captivating by the unknown elements of the puzzle: how did the folder do this? Where are the corners? Is it from a single, uncut square? How large was the square? How in the world did the folder come up with the vision for this piece? What was this design based upon? What was the inspiration? How young or old is the folder? What is this person really like? What is the paper? Who made it? What fiber was used? What types of pigments were used? The display area should make it comfortable for the viewer to contemplate the art while asking these questions.

LIGHTING THE ORIGAMI ART ON DISPLAY

Origami never seems to be properly lit. Even in our own gallery, most origami models are small, and often covered by glass or acrylic. This creates glare and reflections that distract from the beauty of the piece. Origami models have certain folds that should be highlighted with shadow, and others that should be softened with back-lighting. Many origami objects are folded from pure white paper, such as watercolor paper, which can be extremely difficult to light or photograph. The Peabody Essex Museum's Origami NOW! show has displayed origami perhaps better than most other venues, giving each piece plenty of breathing space, and pouring on the light from many angles.

Proper lighting makes all the difference, highlighting these brightly colored Origami Munich Orchid Blossoms and the iridescent mica on the Alexander Aztec Swallowtail Butterflies on display at the Peabody Essex Museum, Salem, Massachusetts.

A comfortable viewing space enhances an exhibit of geometric origami sculptures at the Fitchburg Art Museum.

Like variants often relate well to each other on display. These are origami buds designed and folded by Jeannine Moseley, as displayed at the Peabody Essex Museum, Salem, Massachusetts.

This eleven-foot wide Origamido Butterfly hangs in a 40 foot high glassed-in atrium at the Origami NOW! exhibit, Peabody Essex Museum, Salem, Massachusetts.

PROJECTS

AMERICAN LOBSTER

Designed by Michael G. LaFosse

Michael was inspired by the wet-folding qualities of Elephant Hide™ paper. The color, texture, and hardness of the paper seemed perfect for an origami lobster. Even the thinnest available paper of this type is too thick to fold much detail, such as legs.

Michael savored boiled lobsters when his family took vacations on Cape Cod. It seemed somehow more respectful to carefully extract the succulent meat without destroying the remarkable shell, and Michael became quite skilled at reassembling his lobster's exoskeleton after each dining experience.

Paper Suggestions:

Elephant Hide™, Wyndstone™ or similar stiff, glossy, wet-foldable art papers work best. Use a square of at least 10 inches for the first one you fold.

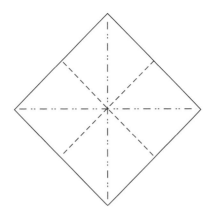

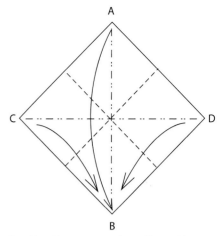

1. Begin white side up if using origami paper. Pre-crease: Diagonal mountain folds and edge-to-edge valley folds.

2. Use the creases to collapse the paper. See figure three for the shape.

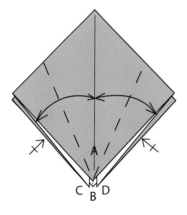

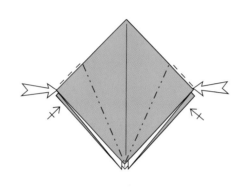

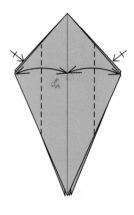

3. Fold the indicated edges to the center crease. Repeat behind.

4. Inside-reverse fold the indicated corners. Repeat behind.

5. Fold the obtuse corners of the kite to meet at the crease, forming creases parallel to the center line. Unfold. Repeat behind.

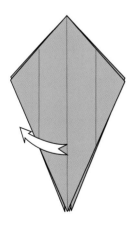

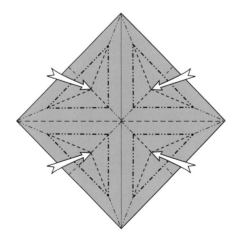

6. Open the paper completely.

7. Using the creases, sink the indicated triangular areas and collapse the paper. Look to figure eight for the shape.

8. Fold up the front corner, as far as it can go.

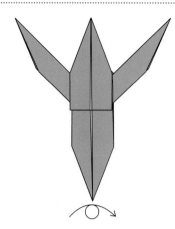

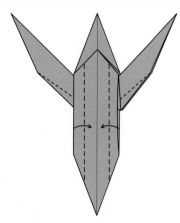

9. Inside-reverse fold the left and right flaps to form the front appendages. Look at figure ten for the angle. Notice that the long, top edge of each flap intersects an obtuse corner of the front flap.

10. Turn over.

11. Fold the left and right edges of the front flap inward and parallel to the center crease. The top layers of the front appendages will form squash folds. See figure twelve.

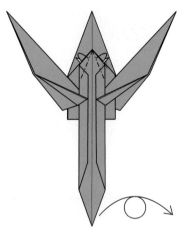

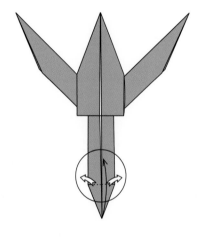

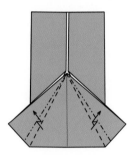

12. Mountain-fold the indicated edges of the upper central corner. Turn over.

13. Open the top layers of the bottom corner. This will form the tail fins.

14. Valley and mountain-fold the outer layers of the pentagonal flap.

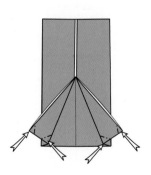

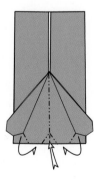

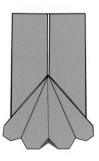

15. Inside-reverse fold the indicated corners to round off the tail fins.

16. Mountain-fold the outer bottom corners to hide them. Mountain-fold the tail and inside-reverse fold the end at the center line.

17. The finished set of tail fins.

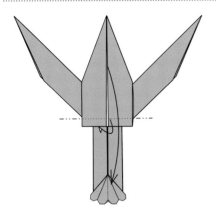

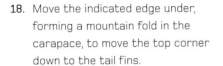

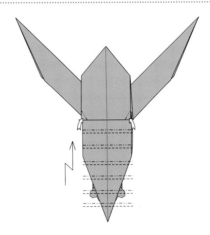

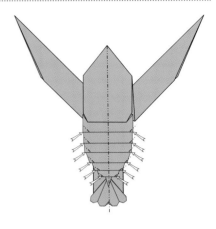

18. Move the indicated edge under, forming a mountain fold in the carapace, to move the top corner down to the tail fins.

19. Inside-reverse fold the bottom corners of the carapace. Form segments in the tail with a series of mountain and valley folds.

20. Inside-reverse fold the square corners of the outer edges of the tail. Softly mountain-fold the model in half.

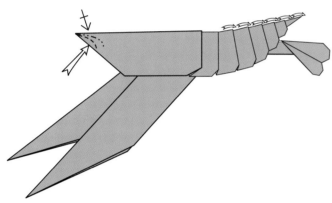

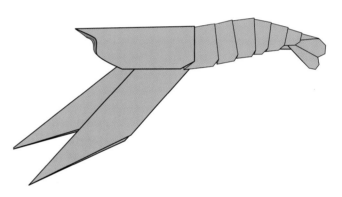

21. Stretch and curve the tail by pulling on the top edge, segment by segment, until the last segment reaches the end of the tail fins. Use curving mountain and valley-folds to form recesses at the front of the carapace.

22. Your model should look like this.

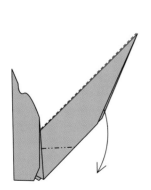

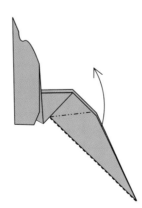

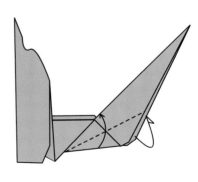

23. Top right view. Inside-reverse fold backward.

24. Inside-reverse fold forward.

25. Fold top and bottom layers over to narrow the base of the arm.

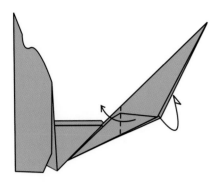

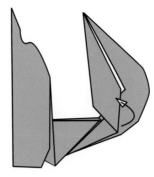

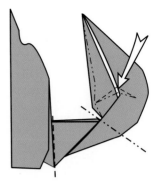

26. Outside-reverse fold to form the claw.

27. Move the hidden layer to the outside.

28. Valley-fold at the base of the arm, near the carapace. Mountain-fold at the base of the claw. Mountain-fold the inner edge of the claw to narrow the thumb. Sink at the base of the thumb. Repeat all arm and claw shaping on the other side.

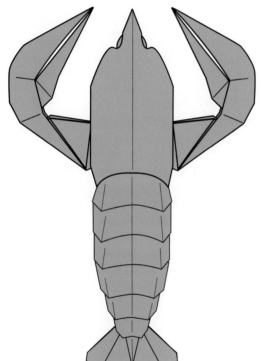

29. The American Lobster.

MONK SEAL FOR LINDA

Designed by Michael G. LaFosse

During our first trips to Hawaii, we enjoyed seeing a pair of endangered Monk Seals at the Honolulu Aquarium. These magnificent creatures dive deep to feed, and are often victims of sharks. When one of our advanced students, Linda Haltinner of Vermont, came for a lesson, she asked to gain some insight into how Michael designs an origami subject. The product of that recent lesson was this Monk Seal, named for Linda.

Paper Suggestions:

Elephant Hide™, Wyndstone™ or similar stiff, wet-foldable art papers work best. Use a square of at least 10 inches for the first one you fold. We suggest you practice this using standard origami paper or foil. When you wet-fold this model, keep the paper a bit on the dry side to keep the larger, unfolded areas clean and strong. The larger your model, the thicker the paper should be.

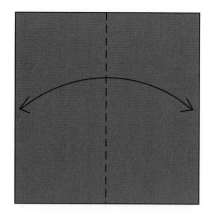

1. Fold in half, edge to edge. Unfold.

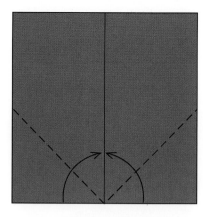

2. Fold up the bottom left and right edges, meeting at the center.

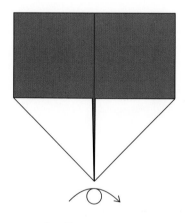

3. Turn over.

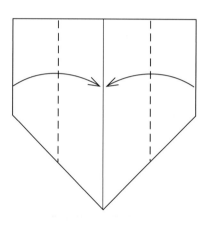

4. Fold in the left and right edges to meet at the center.

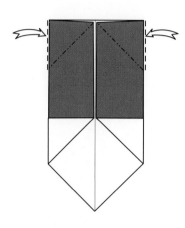

5. Inside-reverse fold the top corners.

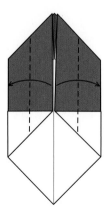

6. Fold the center edges out to match the outer edges. Form squash folds at the top. See figure seven for the shape.

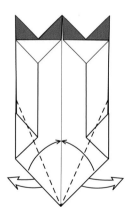

7. Fold the indicated bottom edges to the center. Allow the back layers to move to the front.

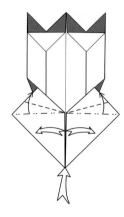

8. Pull open the bottom corner. Crimp the left and right corners above (front flippers.) Look at figure nine for the shape.

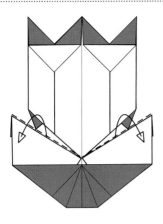

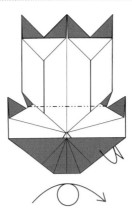

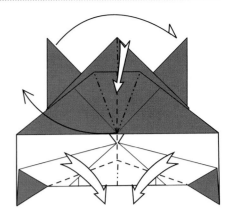

9. Move the back layers of the front flippers to the front.

10. Mountain-fold. Turn over.

11. Outside-reverse fold the front layer while folding the model in half, forming the neck. Sink the indicated layer for the head.

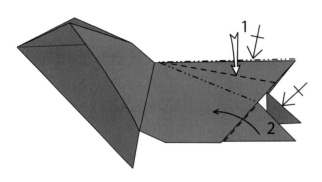

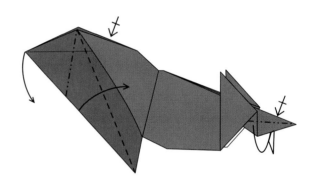

12. Crimp the back (1). Fold up the hind flippers (2).

13. Crimp the front. Mountain-fold the bottom edges of the tail.

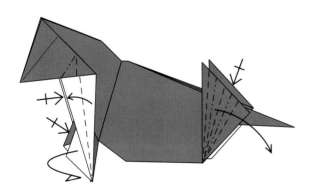

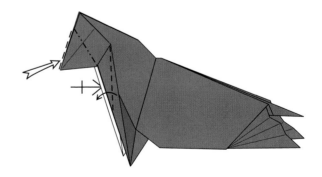

14. Inside-reverse fold the indicated edges of the neck area. Fold the exposed paper of the front flippers behind. Fan-fold the hind flippers and move them down.

15. Inside-reverse fold the jaw. Valley-fold the indicated edge of the neck paper forward, forming a curved line down to the front flippers.

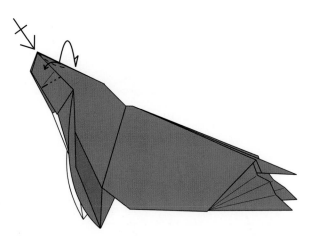

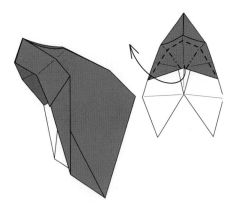

16. Form curved valley folds along the top of the muzzle. Pinch mountain folds at the sides of the muzzle.

17. Side and lower-front view of the head. Fold out and shape the lower jaw.

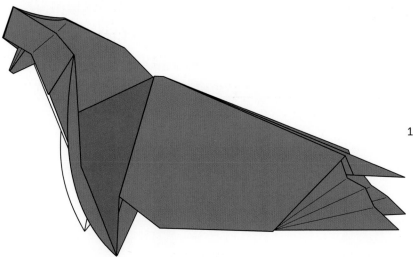

18. The Monk Seal for Linda.

GRACKLE

Designed by Michael G. LaFosse

This origami model is one of the most elegant perched birds. The stance, attitude, proportions, and even the economy of folding make this model one of our favorites. We make paper with black pigment, and then add violet and bronze mica before forming the sheets. Michael designed this model after watching the local grackles strut along the tidal beach of the Merrimack River in front of our house.

Paper Suggestions:

Use black or dark purple back-coated washi or lightweight art paper. The paper may be painted with a light wash of iridescent purple acrylic for a lifelike effect. A 10 to 12-inch square will produce a nice sized model. Ordinary 10-inch origami paper or foil work well for practice.

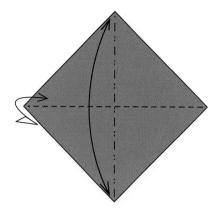

1. Valley-fold in half horizontally, and mountain-fold in half vertically.

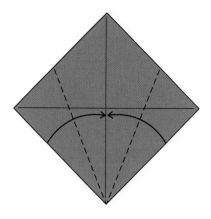

2. Valley-fold the bottom left and right edges to meet at the center mountain crease.

3. Turn over.

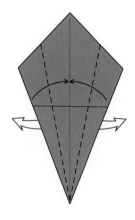

4. Valley-fold the long edges to meet at the center. Allow the hidden corners to come to the front.

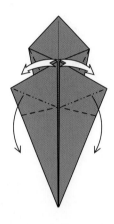

5. Using the pre-existing mountain creases, move the indicated corners down as far as possible, flat.

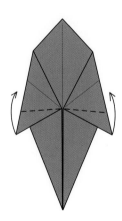

6. Valley-fold each corner up.

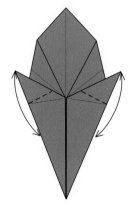

7. Valley-fold corners down, aligning the outer edges together. Unfold.

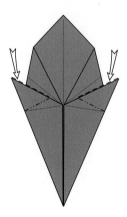

8. Inside-reverse fold.

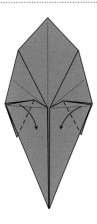

9. Fold top layers over.

10. Inside-reverse fold the indicated edges of each square.

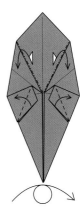

11. Mountain-fold along the V-shaped area at the top. Unfold. Fold the indicated corners outward. Turn Over.

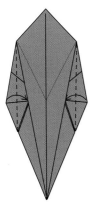

12. Valley-fold the outside corners in, matching the edges.

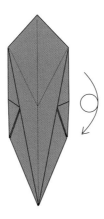

13. Turn over, top to bottom.

14. Valley-fold the inside edges out as far as possible, flat.

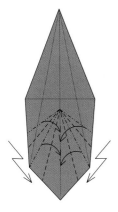

15. Using the mountain crease as a guide, install a series of valley and mountain folds to narrow the tail.

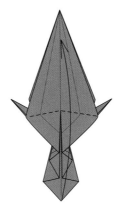

16. Valley-fold the tail up. Look to figure seventeen for the shape.

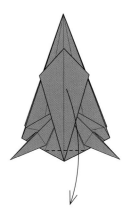

17. Valley-fold across the bottom corner, between the creases, to bring the tail back down.

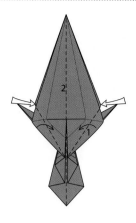

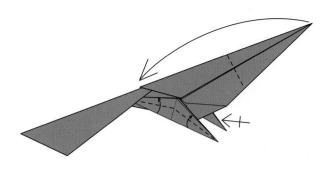

18. (1) Valley-fold the indicated edges inward. Use the back layer corners, indicated by the white arrows, as guides. (2) Valley-fold in half, length-wise.

19. Outside-reverse fold the front point to the back corner of the body to form the neck. Valley-fold the outside bottom edge of the leg paper. Repeat behind.

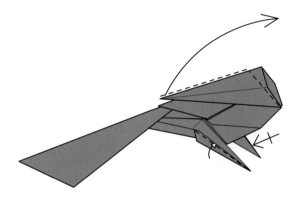

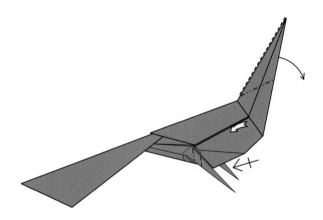

20. Outside-reverse fold the neck point forward and upward. Valley-fold the exposed paper in the leg to narrow the shape further. Repeat behind.

21. Inside-reverse fold the top point of the neck downward. Pull out and round the trapped layer of paper along the side of the body. Install two complimentary inside-reverse folds to make the joints in the leg. Repeat behind.

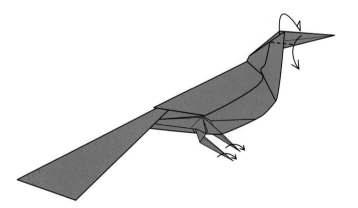

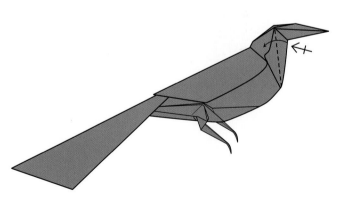

22. Outside-reverse fold the top of the head. Curve the ends of the legs for the feet.

23. Valley-fold the outermost layer of paper in the neck. Repeat behind.

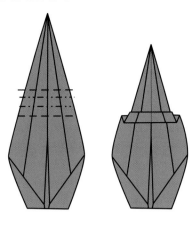
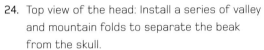

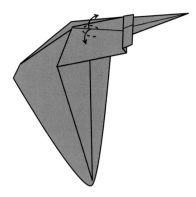

24. Top view of the head: Install a series of valley and mountain folds to separate the beak from the skull.

25. Open the upper and lower layers on the side of the head, forming an eye. Repeat behind.

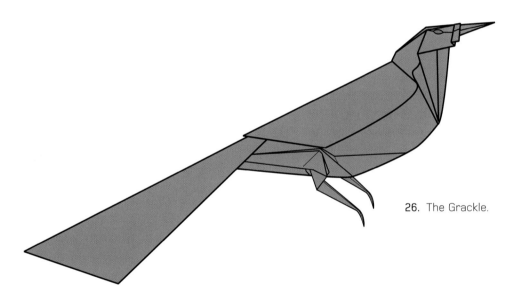

26. The Grackle.

WEST INDIAN MANATEE

Designed by Michael G. LaFosse

Michael's freshman year in college was at the University of Tampa, and several field trips involved observing the diminishing population of manatees. One year before opening the Origamido Studio, Michael and I drove to Florida and spent Christmas watching the Manatees huddled in the warm waters of the power plant just south of the City of Tampa.

Paper Suggestions:

Use back-coated washi, or stiffer art paper with some "tooth" or texture. Use a square of at least 10 inches for the first one you fold. Try making smaller calves for your subsequent tries.

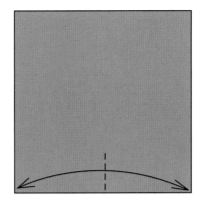

1. Mark the middle of the bottom edge with a short valley crease.

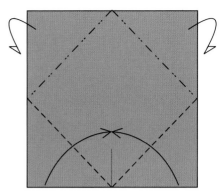

2. Valley-fold the bottom corners to meet at the middle of the paper. Mountain-fold the top corners to the back.

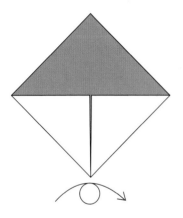

3. Turn over.

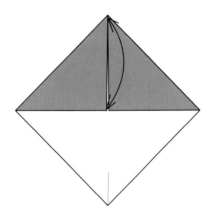

4. Valley-fold the top corner to down to the middle. Unfold.

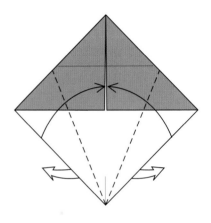

5. Valley-fold the bottom edges to meet at the middle. Allow the hidden corners to come to the front.

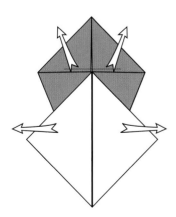

6. Open completely.

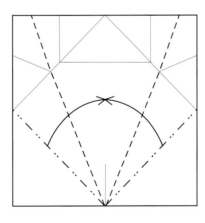

7. Use the indicated creases to mountain and valley-fold the paper closed. Look ahead at figure eight for the shape.

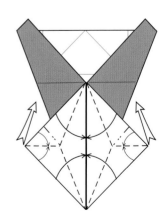

8. Rabbit-ear the square corners of the two triangle flaps.

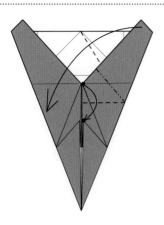

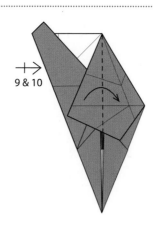

9. Match the two corners indicated by the black dots. Squash-fold.

10. Valley-fold the top layer flap over to the right side of the model. Repeat steps nine and ten on the left side.

11. Valley-fold the square corner of the triangular flap to the left. Lay the end of the indicated crease on the center line to set the angle of the fold.

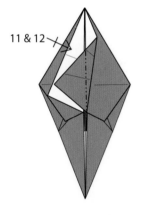

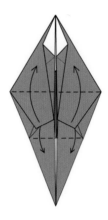

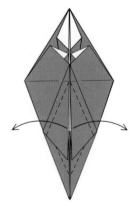

12. Mountain-fold the square corner inside of the model. Repeat steps eleven and twelve on the left side.

13. Valley-fold the upper layer flaps toward the top and the lower corners toward the bottom.

14. Twist the rabbit ear corners out, left and right, forming a square area with the top corner reaching the horizontal crease above it.

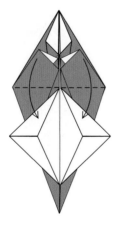

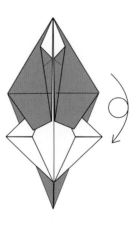

15. Fold the indicated flaps down.

16. Turn over, top to bottom.

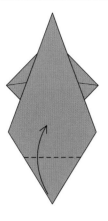

17. Valley-fold the bottom corner up.

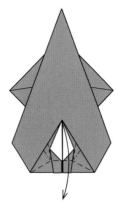

18. Crimp the left and right sides of the flap as you fold the top corner down.

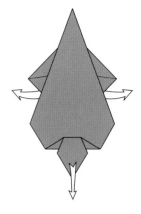

19. Open the paper out to resemble the shape in figure twenty.

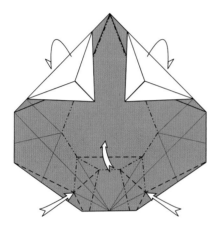

20. Use the indicated crease pattern to collapse the paper, reorganizing the layers in the tail.

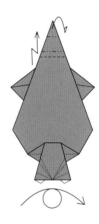

21. Mountain and valley-fold the top corner to form the head. Turn over.

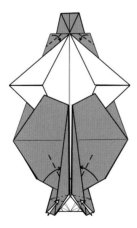

22. Valley-fold the corners at the base of the head in. Crimp the tail to clean up the excess paper. Round and narrow the body by valley-folding the indicated bottom edges under the vertical center layers. Notice that the valley folds are short.

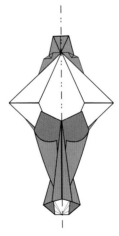

23. Softly valley-fold the model in half.

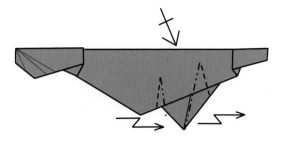

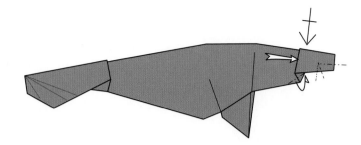

24. Crimp the paper just behind and at the leading edge of the flipper. Repeat on the other side.

25. Crimp the front of the muzzle into a box-like shape. Suggest an eye by making a dent in the folded edge at the back of the muzzle.

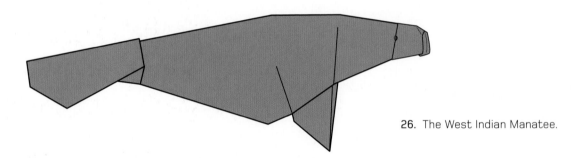

26. The West Indian Manatee.

CORMORANT

Designed by Michael G. LaFosse

Just down the Merrimack River there are rock outcroppings where cormorants rest and dry their wings. We often see them fishing the deeper channel outside our house, and they work hard to swim against the current where the fish travel. One of the best places to see cormorants is on the rocks in Amesbury, behind the house where Li'l Abner's cartoonist, Al Capp once lived. Just ask, the locals will know!

Paper Suggestions:

Dyed washi or art papers work best for smaller models. Use stiffer paper, or back coat the washi to stiffer stock when making larger models. Start with a square of at least 10 inches.

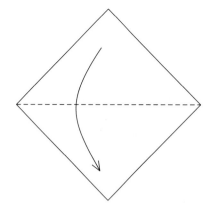

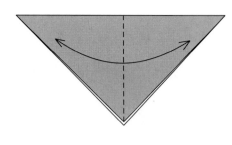

1. Valley-fold in half, corner-to-corner, color on the outside if using standard origami paper.

2. Valley-fold in half, corner to corner. Unfold.

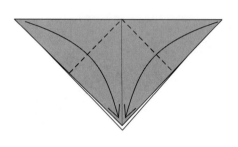

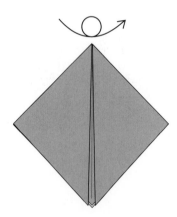

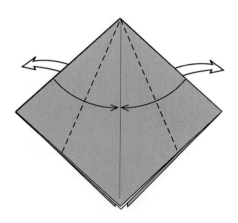

3. Valley-fold the top corners down to the square corner at the bottom.

4. Turn over, left to right.

5. Valley-fold the top two folded edges to meet in the middle. Allow the hidden corners to come to the front.

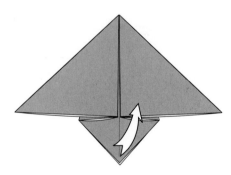

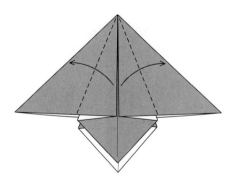

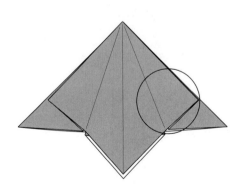

6. Pull out the trapped layers so that they lay on the top of the model.

7. Valley-fold the middle two edges out to meet the outer edges of the model.

8. Detail view for step nine.

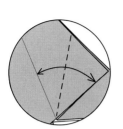 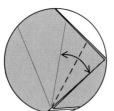 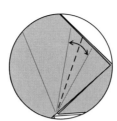

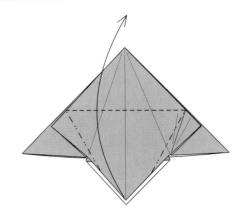

9. Install this series of creases to mark the level for the petal fold to follow.

10. Petal-fold.

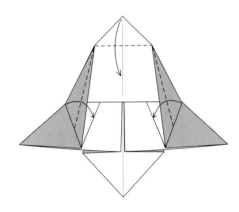

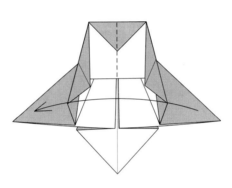

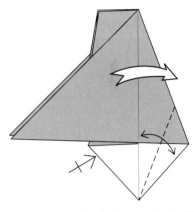

11. Valley-fold the top corner down at the level of the tips of the triangular shaped layers. Valley-fold side corners in to touch the folded edge indicated.

12. Move the right side flap to the left.

13. Pre-crease the bottom edge to the center line. Unfold and move the flap back to the right.

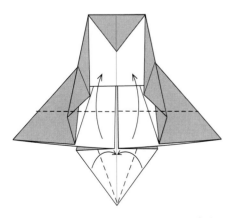

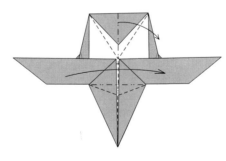

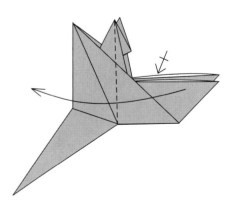

14. Valley-fold the bottom edges of the flaps up. Layers below will follow. Use the pre-creases from the previous step to petal-fold the bottom corner.

15. Valley-fold the model in half. Inside-reverse fold the top edge to form the legs and outside-reverse fold the bottom corner to form the neck.

16. Fold the wing flaps over the body.

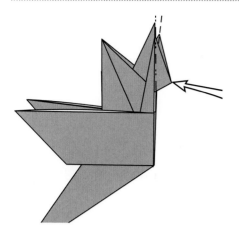

17. Inside-reverse fold the exposed paper to narrow the legs.

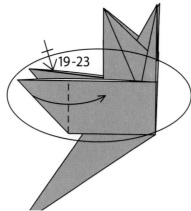

18. Valley-fold wing tip over. Repeat behind.

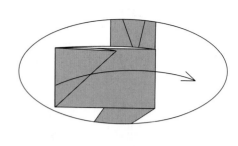

19. Move wing to work from the other side.

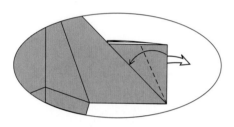

20. Valley-fold outer edge in to meet the folded edge on the top of the wing.

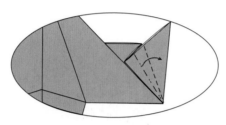

21. Squash-fold.

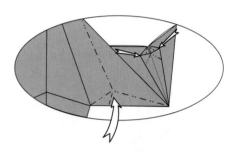

22. Inside-reverse fold the end corners of the squash fold. Inside-reverse fold the edge of the wing to form the elbow. Mountain-fold along the back edge of the wing, beginning at the bend in the elbow.

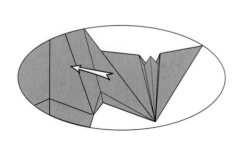

23. Shape the wing evenly. Repeat steps nineteen through twenty-three on the other wing.

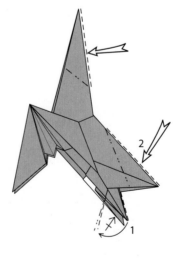

24. Inside-reverse fold the top of the neck to form the head. (1) Inside-reverse fold the legs to form the feet. (2) Inside-reverse fold the back to form the tail.

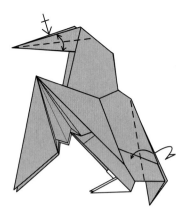

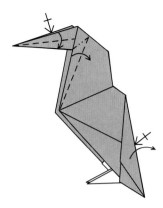

25. Pre-crease the long point of the head by valley-folding the top edges down to the bottom edge, one on each side. Unfold. Valley-fold the edges of the tail to the outside of the body.

26. Valley-fold the leading edge of the neck back, bringing the top edges of the beak down at the same time. Free the trapped layer of paper on the outside of the tail. (Wings hidden for clarity.)

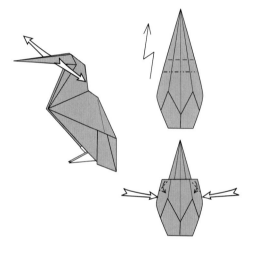

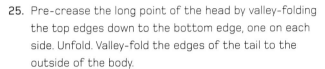

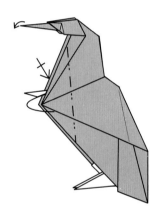

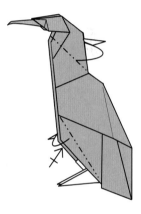

27. Open the paper in the beak. View from the top: Mountain and valley-fold the beak. Valley-fold the resulting corners in the head for eyes. Close up the head and beak.

28. Curve the tip of the beak. Mountain-fold the indicated corners into the body.

29. Mountain-fold the lower edges into the body. Twist the neck slightly.

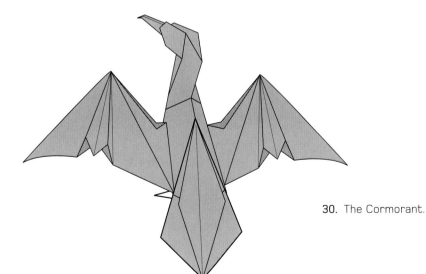

30. The Cormorant.

HUMPBACK WHALE

Designed by Michael G. LaFosse

The Cumming family of South Groveland, Massachusetts has folded with us since the beginning of the Origamido Studio. Rocky Cumming had spent quite a bit of time out on the Atlantic, and often marveled at the Humpbacks. Rocky and his daughter, Emily, have been folding Michael's origami Koi for many years, and Emily has even taught others how to fold the model at the NYC origami convention. Rocky's conversations with Michael about the whales motivated Michael to refine his earlier modifications of his design for a humpback whale, but the scale of the model always bothered him. One day, Rocky showed up at the studio carrying a 5 foot roll of watercolor paper. We proceeded to make some black pulp for the back, and added gray pulp to form patches on the belly, while the backing watercolor paper was dampened on the 6 foot square glass table. In all, Rocky folded three of the Humpbacks for display at the Origami USA Convention in New York City. He left another piece of paper for Michael to fold.

Paper Suggestions:

Use black and white duo washi for this model. Use paper at least 5 inches square. We make large sheets by spraying paper pulp onto a cloth. Pulp spraying is an unusual papermaking technique, requiring special equipment and studio facilities. Since this is more difficult we also produce large sheets by transferring smaller, couched sheets of pulp from the papermaking screen onto a large, wet felt. The individual sheets will bond together when you leave 1/2 to 1 inch of overlap, and pound the seams smooth with a wooden mallet, or flatten them with a paint roller.

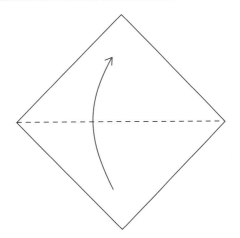

1.   Begin white side up. Valley-fold in half, bottom corner to top.

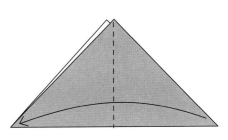

2.   Valley-fold in half.

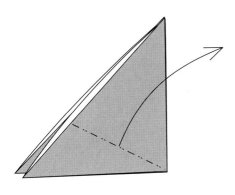

3.   Squash-fold. Look to figure four for the angle.

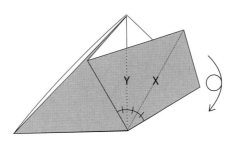

4.   Notice that crease X and line Y would divide the angle of the folded corner into equal thirds. Turn over, top to bottom.

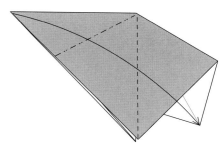

5.   Squash-fold to match.

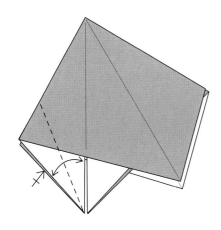

6.   Pre-crease for a petal fold by moving the bottom raw edge to the nearby folded edge. Unfold. Repeat behind.

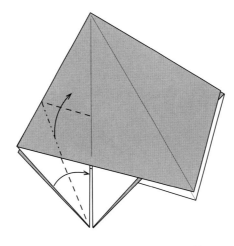

7.   Petal-fold up the pre-creased layer.

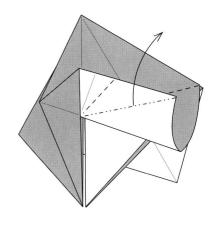

8.   Mountain-fold from the center to the outer corner and move the corner up. Flatten the corner.

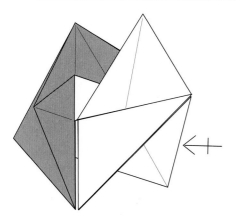

9. Repeat behind.

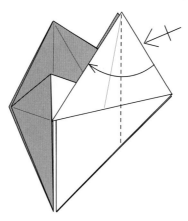

10. Valley-fold the outer edge to the folded edge. Repeat behind.

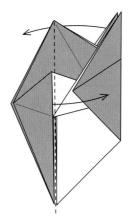

11. Rearrange the layers. Look to figure twelve for the shape.

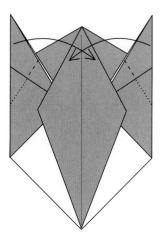

12. Fold the exposed corners inward to cross each other. Notice that the fold extends deep under the covering layer.

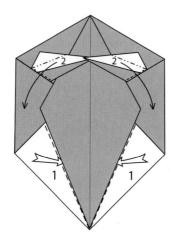

13. (1) Valley-fold the bottom edges under the top layers to meet at the middle. (2) Squash-fold the fins to point backward.

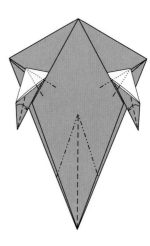

14. Expose the white color on the fins by valley-folding the indicated layer over. Inside-reverse fold the bottom corners together to form the tail.

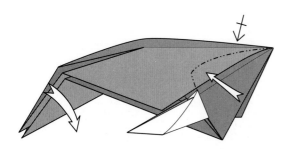

15. Separate the two layers of the tail. Install curved mountain-folds in the top layer of the head to shape the upper jaw.

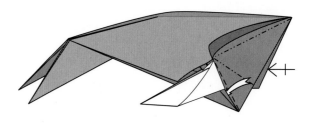

16. Mountain-fold the paper in the lower jaw. Crimp the excess paper into the pocket in front of the pectoral fin. Repeat on the other side.

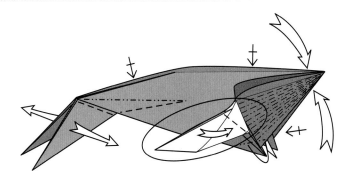

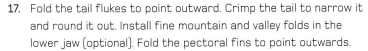

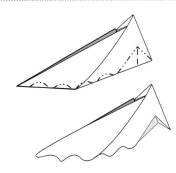

17. Fold the tail flukes to point outward. Crimp the tail to narrow it and round it out. Install fine mountain and valley folds in the lower jaw (optional). Fold the pectoral fins to point outwards.

18. Shape the leading edge of the fins with a series of rounded dents.

19. Detail view of the flukes.

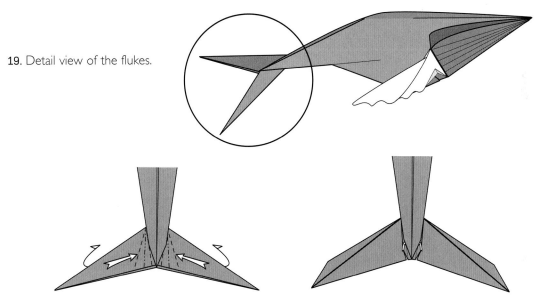

20. Crimp the top layer close to the tail. Swivel the top layer to form an extra edge.

21. Tuck the exposed paper of the crimp under the tail to lock and hide.

22. The Humpback Whale.

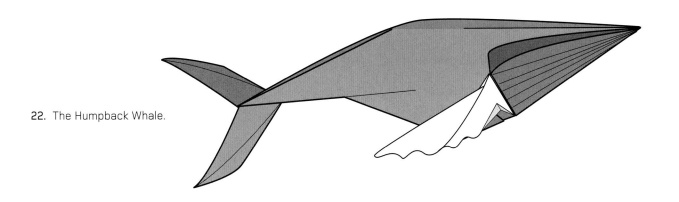

PENGUIN

Designed by Michael G. LaFosse

This is one of Michael's earliest original origami creations. He recalls fiddling with a church flier during Mass, working out the basic plan that would become this origami Penguin. Later, he tried the design from a piece of duo origami paper. Surprisingly, the Penguin came out with a white body and black belly. He quickly turned the paper over and refolded what has become this delightful origami classic.

Paper Suggestions:

Use black and white duo washi for this model. Use paper at least 10 inches square. Regular 10-inch origami paper also works well, especially for practice, but apply only small amounts of moisture with a damp sponge, just along the lines you will be creasing.

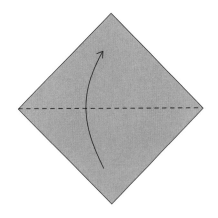

1. Begin with the black side up. Valley-fold in half, bottom corner to top.

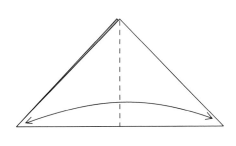

2. Valley-fold in half and unfold.

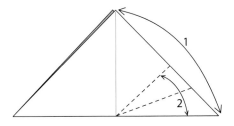

3. (1) Fold the bottom right corner to the top corner. Unfold. (2) Fold the right half of the bottom edge to the crease above. Unfold.

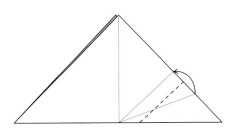

4. Valley-fold, matching the two crease ends of the previous folds.

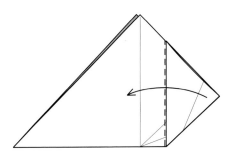

5. Valley-fold along the vertical folded edge.

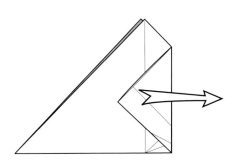

6. Unfold.

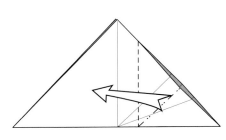

7. Squash-fold.

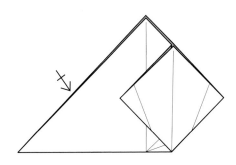

8. Repeat on the left.

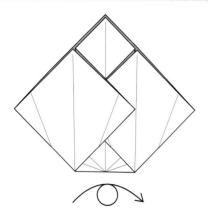

9. Your paper should look like this. Turn over.

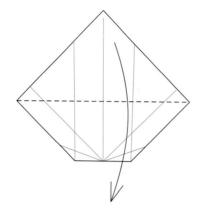

10. Valley-fold the top corner down as far as it will go.

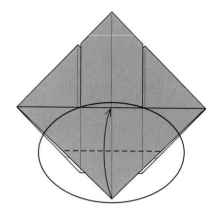

11. Valley-fold the bottom corner up to touch the middle of the folded edge above.

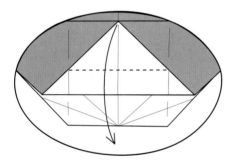

12. Valley-fold the corner down at the level of the outside vertical creases.

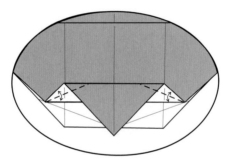

13. Pre-crease for an inside-reverse fold, matching the left and right raw edges to the folded edge, below. Unfold.

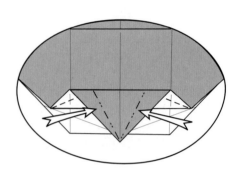

14. Inside-reverse fold to narrow the paper for the tail.

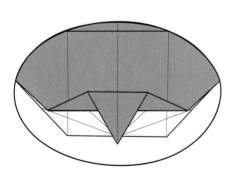

15. Your paper should look like this.

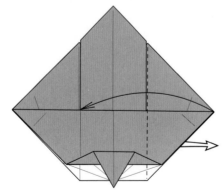

16. Valley-fold the right corner flap to the left. Allow the hidden corner to come to the front.

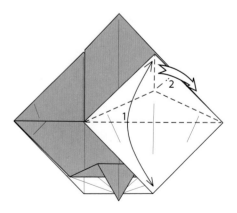

17. (1) Valley-fold the top corner down to the bottom. Unfold. (2) rabbit-ear the top corner to form the wing.

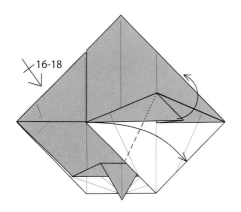

18. Swivel the wing to point up and move the left corner of the rabbit-ear down to touch the lower outer edge. Repeat steps sixteen through eighteen on the left side.

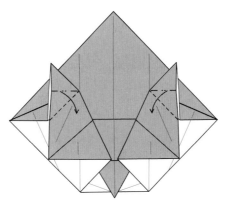

19. Squash-fold the wings.

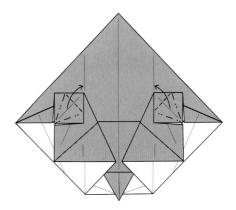

20. Petal-fold the wings.

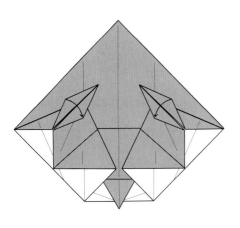

21. Valley-fold the wings in half.

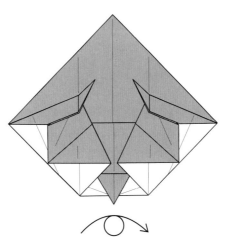

22. Turn over.

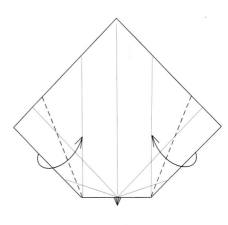

23. Valley-fold the lower outer edges to their nearest vertical crease.

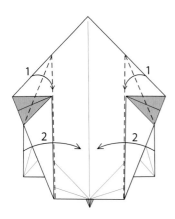

24. (1) Valley-fold the indicated portion of the edge to the vertical crease. (2) Valley-fold along the vertical creases to bring the outer areas in.

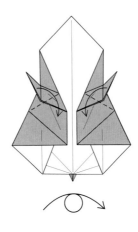

25. Valley-fold the wings down. Turn over.

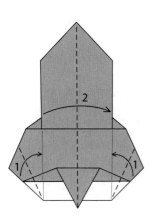

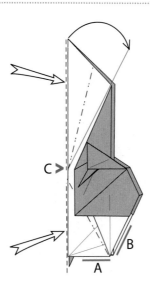

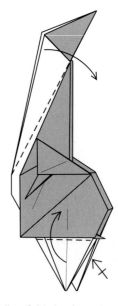

26. (1) Valley-fold the lower left and right edges into the vertical creases. (2) Valley-fold in half.

27. Inside-reverse fold the top corner, stopping at point C where the paper begins to get thick. The angle is set by matching the folded edge with the top black corners. (2) Inside-reverse fold the bottom white corner. Align the edges marked A with edges marked B.

28. Valley-fold the front layer of the neck over to reveal the inside. Add some more moisture where these layers build up considerable thickness. Valley-fold the bottom white corners up, forming the feet, folding along each edge of black paper.

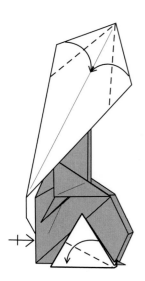

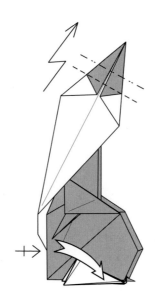

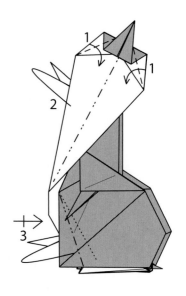

29. Valley-fold the short edges of the white kite shape to the middle crease. Valley-fold the back edges of the lower white triangle to the bottom, forming the feet.

30. Valley and mountain-fold the top corner for the beak. Move the trapped layer of black paper to the front to cover and lock the foot. Repeat behind.

31. (1) Valley-fold the short edges of the head in. (2) Mountain fold the neck in half. (3) Tuck the front edges of the black layer into the front of the body to complete the paper lock on the feet.

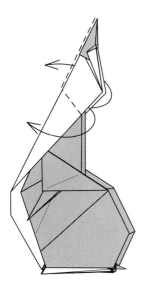

32. Outside-reverse fold the head.

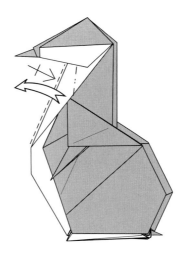

33. Swivel the layers of paper in the neck to re-shape the chest.

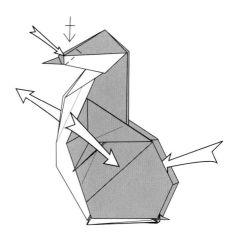

34. Inside-reverse fold the corners at the front of the head for the eyes. Push out from the inside to expand the model, opening the chest and belly. Mountain-fold the back edges into the body.

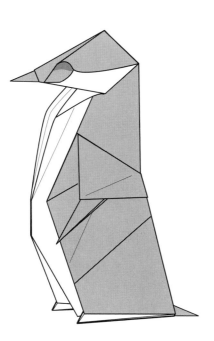

35. Side view.

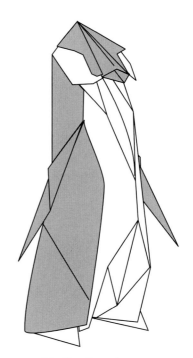

36. The Penguin.

BANANA SLUG

Designed by Michael G. LaFosse

The Banana Slug is the mascot for the University of California at Santa Cruz's athletic teams, selected to counter the fiercely competitive choices of other schools. Mollusks are Michael's second passion. Here is a guy who used to claim to have memorized at least 10,000 Latin binomials for gastropods and bivalves. But not all mollusks have shells, and one of the most beautifully artistic patterns in nature is found on the backs of the common garden slugs. These bright, slimy creatures are so different from human beings, just imagine if we ever discover life on another planet as interesting as a mollusk, then maybe people will take more time to observe these remarkable creatures here on Earth. Michael started folding garden slugs when he observed them getting the jump on our zucchini plants.

Paper Suggestions:

Use yellow and brown duo washi for this model. Use paper at least 7 inches square.

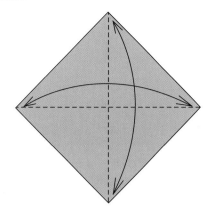

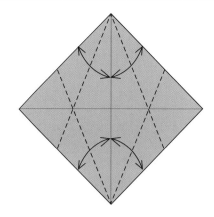

1. Begin with the wrong side up if using duo colored paper. Valley-fold in half diagonally both ways.

2. One at a time, valley-fold each of the four edges of the square to the center and unfold.

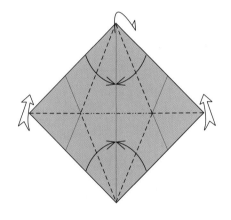

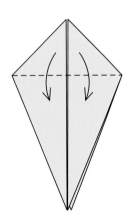

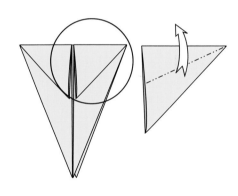

3. Rabbit-ear the left and right corners. Move the top corner to the back and to the bottom.

4. Valley-fold the two top corners down.

5. (Detail of eyestalk follows.) Squash-fold the top right corner.

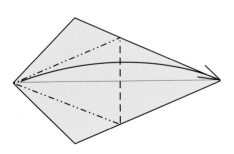

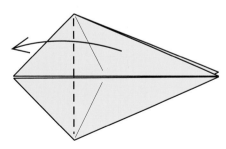

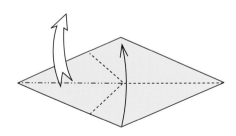

6. Petal-fold.

7. Move the petal corner to the left.

8. Valley-fold the diamond shape in half, bottom to top, and inside-reverse fold the petal corner straight up to form the eyestalk.

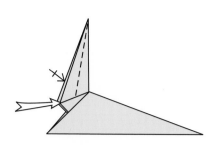

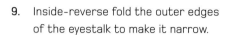

9. Inside-reverse fold the outer edges of the eyestalk to make it narrow.

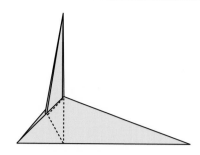

10. Your paper should look like this.

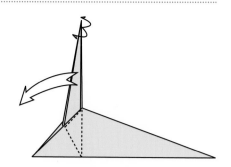

11. Pull the eyestalk to the left to change the angle. Outside-reverse fold the layers at the tip of the eyestalk to form the eye and to change the color (if using duo paper).

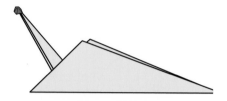

12. The completed eyestalk and eye. Repeat steps 5 through 11 on the other side.

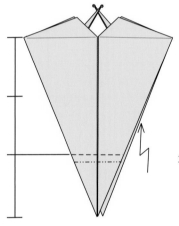

13. Valley and mountain fold the bottom third of the front flap.

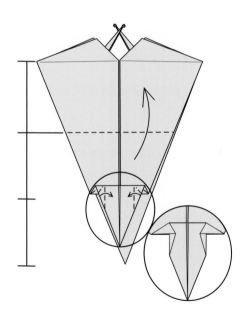

14. Valley-fold and squash to narrow the point. Notice that the valleys are parallel to the center crease. Valley-fold the bottom two thirds of the flap up.

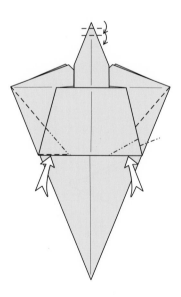

15. Valley-fold the tip of the top point over twice. Inside-reverse fold the two indicated corners. Note the shape carefully as each side is different.

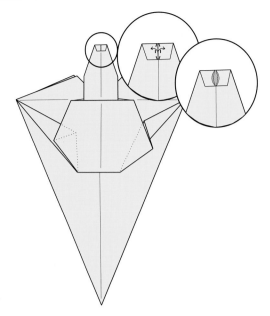

16. Detail: Open the mouth by moving the two raw edges away from the center.

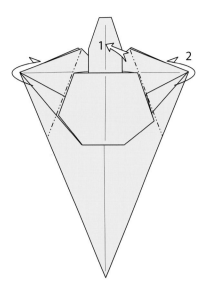

17. (1) Tuck the top flap under the two eyestalks. (2) Mountain-fold the sides under.

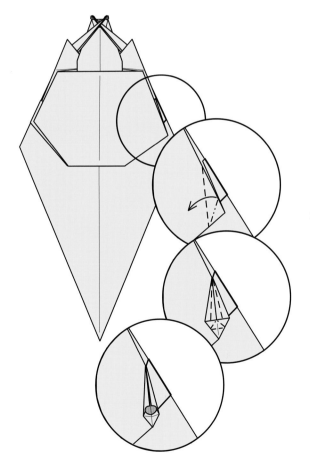

18. Detail: Form the breathing pore in the mantle by first squash-folding the indicated corner on the right side. Petal-fold to narrow the long edges. Form a circular opening at the back end of the petal fold.

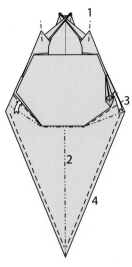

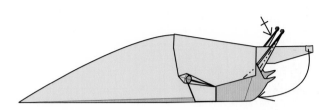

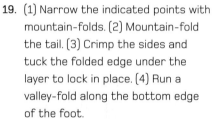

19. (1) Narrow the indicated points with mountain-folds. (2) Mountain-fold the tail. (3) Crimp the sides and tuck the folded edge under the layer to lock in place. (4) Run a valley-fold along the bottom edge of the foot.

20. Pinch the eyestalks in half to narrow them further. Curve the front flap over and down to move the mouth under the front of the model.

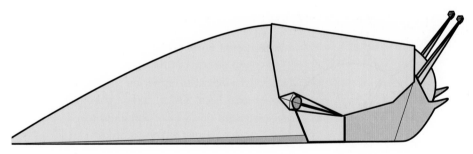

21. The Banana Slug.

BIRDWING BUTTERFLY

Designed by Michael G. LaFosse

Michael was one of the Guest Artists at the Folding Australia convention in Melbourne, Australia in 2007. While there, we visited the Melbourne Museum, and snapped some photos near the exhibits of Birdwing Butterflies with incredibly beautiful, geometric markings. These creatures are found only in the Southern Hemisphere, and their long forewings give them quite a distinctive shape. This particular pattern most closely resembles several species of the genus, Triodes, found in Malaysia. This is just one recent example of butterflies and moths that Michael designs using the system of mixing and matching variables at key steps in the design. We presented this technique in our recent book, The LaFosse Butterfly System: A Field of Discovery (Origamido, Inc.).

Paper Suggestions:

Use black and iridescent green duo washi for this model. It is easy to make duo papers suitable for this model by merely painting an iridescent green airbrush pigment onto black washi. Use paper at least 10 inches square.

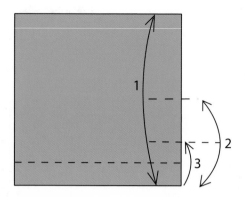

1. Begin with the green side up. (1) Mark the center of the right edge with a short valley-fold. (2) Make a short valley crease to mark the distance half way between the bottom edge and the valley crease above. (3) Valley-fold the bottom edge up to the lowest crease.

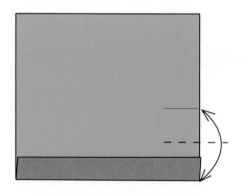

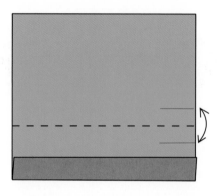

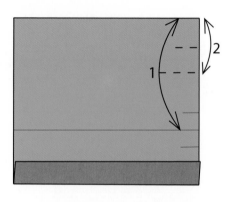

2. Make a short valley crease to mark the distance halfway from the bottom folded edge to the valley crease above.

3. Valley-fold, matching the lower valley crease to the upper valley crease.

4. (1) Make a short valley crease to mark the distance halfway from the top edge to the full length valley crease below. (2) Make a short valley crease to mark the distance half way between the top edge and the short valley crease below.

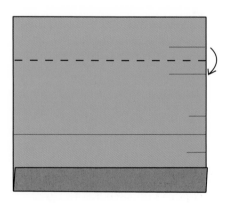

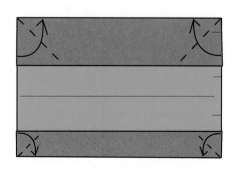

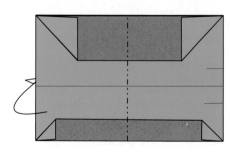

5. Valley-fold, matching the upper valley crease to the lower.

6. Valley-fold each of the four free corner flaps to the outer edges.

7. Mountain-fold in half.

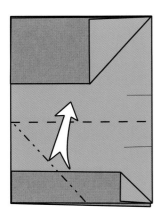

8. Squash-fold.

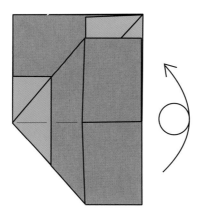

9. Turn over top to bottom.

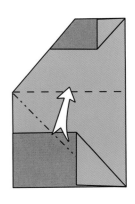

10. Squash-fold.

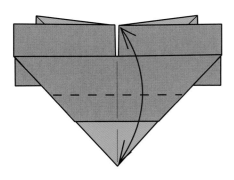

11. Valley-fold the bottom corner up to the top of the gap. Unfold.

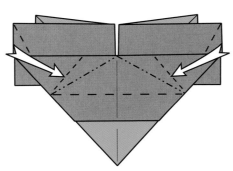

12. Inside-reverse fold the left and right halves of the top layer, forming a point at the center of the edge.

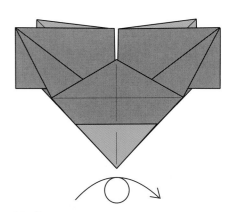

13. Turn over.

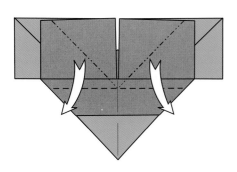

14. Squash-fold the left and right halves to form the wings.

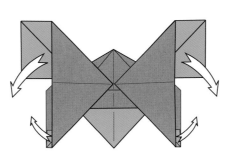

15. Pull out the indicated corners as far as they will go, flat.

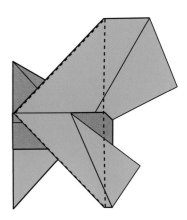

16. Top layer removed for an X-ray view of the result of the previous step.

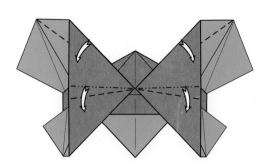

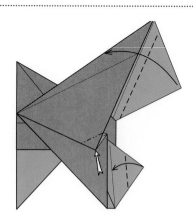

17. Crimp the middle of the top layer of each wing down, swiveling the leading edge over and stopping at the outer top corner.

18. Valley-fold the top corner to touch the leading edge of the wing. The Valley fold should be made parallel to the nearby raw edge. Inside-reverse fold the indicated corner where the fore and hind wings separate. Valley-fold in the lower wing corner to touch the crease.

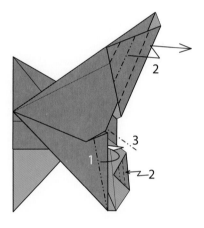

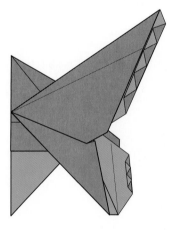

19. (1) Mountain-fold. (2) Valley and mountain-fold the triangles to form the pattern of alternating colored triangles. (3) Mountain-fold this small area of exposed paper.

20. The wings should look like this. Repeat on the left side.

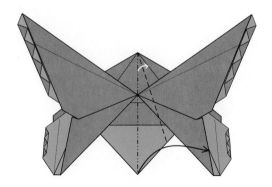

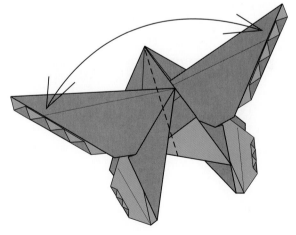

21. Begin to form the body by mountain-folding the middle and swiveling it across the right wing. Make the tip of the abdomen touch the indicated folded edge on the hind wing.

22. Fold the left set of wings over to match. Unfold.

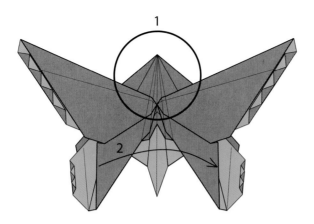

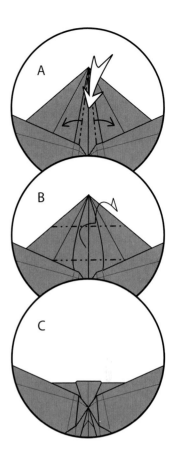

23. (1A) Squash-fold the center keel of paper in the head area to flatten it. (1B) Mountain-fold over and over twice to form the head. (1C) The head should look like this. (2) Bring the wings together with the body between.

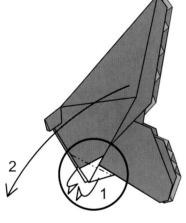

24. (1) Narrow the back end of the abdomen with mountain folds. (2) Open the wings.

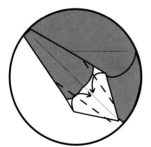

25. The Birdwing Butterfly.

MODULAR FLOWER AND LEAF

Designed by Michael G. LaFosse

Modular flowers have been popular origami subjects at the Origamido Studio. Michael's ingenious tab, pocket, and fold-over locking arrangement yields a huge array of possible flower shapes and styles. Nicely folded origami plants and flowers of handmade papers make great display supports for your finest origami art. We have chosen these models to illustrate the world of compound origami projects and displays—a topic not frequently considered in much detail by other origami authors.

Paper Suggestions:

Use any colors of duo washi for this model. Each blossom will require 6 pieces of paper, 1.5 inches square.

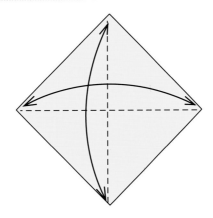

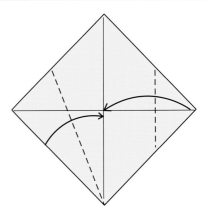

1. The flower uses six squares. Each is folded the same. Begin with the paper wrong side up. Valley-fold in half diagonally both ways.

2. Valley-fold the bottom left edge to the center. Valley-fold the right corner to the center.

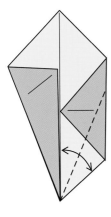

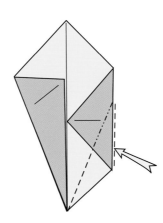

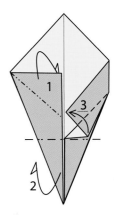

3. Valley-fold the bottom right edge to the center. Unfold.

4. Inside-reverse fold.

5. (1) Mountain-fold the top left corner inside. (2) Mountain-fold the bottom corner up. Notice that the fold should happen at the level of the bottom edge of the inside-reverse fold on the right. (3) Valley-fold the lower flap of the inside-reverse fold up.

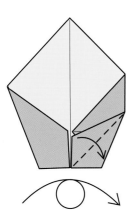

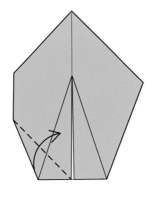

6. Bring the flap back down. Turn over.

7. Valley-fold the bottom left flap up.

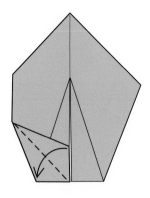

8. Fold the flap back down.

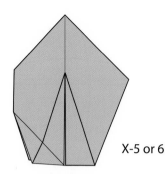

X-5 or 6

9. The finished petal. You will need five to six petals to make one flower.

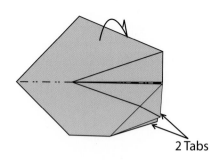

2 Tabs

10. Mountain-fold the petal in half. Notice the two tabs at the bottom right.

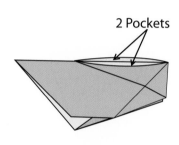

2 Pockets

11. Notice the two pockets at the top edge.

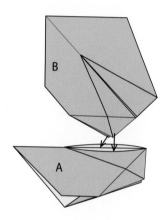

B

A

12. Insert the two tabs from one petal into the two pockets of another.

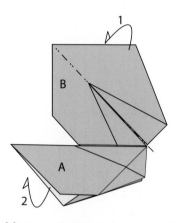

1

B

A

2

13. (1) Mountain-fold the new petal in half. (2) Move the back layer of the first petal up to make the petal full and flat. This locks the two petals together.

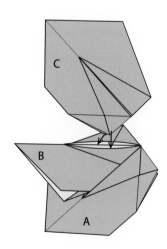

C

B

A

14. Add a new petal in the same manner.

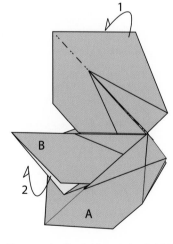

1

B

A

2

15. Be sure to first Mountain-fold the newest petal in half and then open the previous petal, as before.

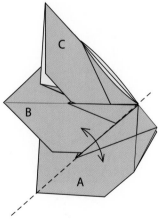

C

B

A

16. One more detail. Place a strong valley crease in the first petal. This will ensure the lock and begin to cup the blossom. Do this to each successive petal as you add new ones.

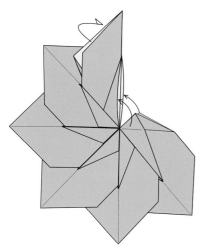

17. Once all of the petals have been locked together you can close the blossom by tucking the tabs of the first petal into the pockets of the last.

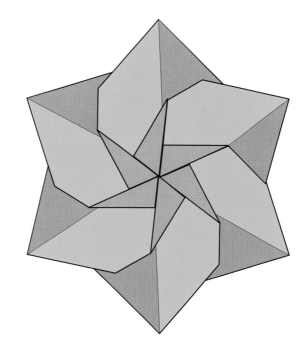

18. The Modular Flower.

LEAF

This simple leaf is a quick and versatile origami element. For best effect, study the size, number and arrangement of leaves on a real plant with similar blossoms. A grouping of origami leaves acts as a frame, and will not only add realism to your flower, it will enhance the display.

Paper Suggestions:

Use back-coated green washi for this model. Use varying sizes of paper, about 2 inches square.

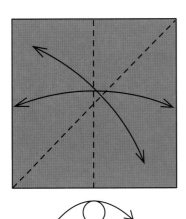

1. Valley-fold in half edge-to-edge once and diagonally once. Turn over.

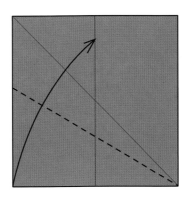

2. Be sure that the crease pattern is oriented as shown in figure two. Valley-fold the bottom left corner up to touch the vertical center crease.

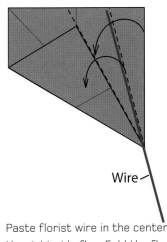

Wire

3. Paste florist wire in the center of the right side flap. Fold the flap over twice.

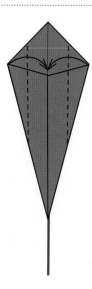

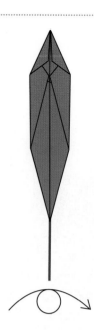

4. Fold the left and right corners of the kite shape to meet at the center. You can make the edges parallel or angled.

5. Fold the top edges to meet at the center.

6. Turn over.

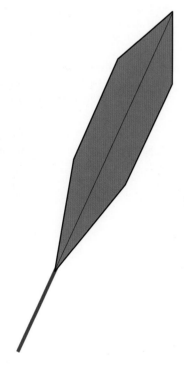

7. The finished leaf. You can curl the leaf or fold in half lengthwise. Refer to the Building Flowers and Plants section of the Techniques chapter for details on floral origami model construction.

POND TURTLE

Designed by Michael G. LaFosse

We have a walking path around the local reservoir where pond turtles can often be seen sunning themselves on the logs or shoreline. Once in a while we will bring one home to study, show to our students, photograph and release. One little slider was so shy, we named her Heidi. Eventually, she became comfortable having us around, and foraged in the grass while getting her picture taken. Once we were walking from our home to the Studio, and found a turtle on the sidewalk in downtown Haverhill. Although the Merrimack River runs right through the city, the turtle had climbed nearly 20 feet out of the river, and its chances for survival on busy Route 110 were slim to none. We released this turtle, named Gene, back into the River in front of my house, in order for him to contribute his genes back to the Merrimack River Gene Pool. Turtles are fascinating creatures. When asked what he wanted to be when he grew up, young Michael LaFosse replied, "A turtle!" He has been observing, sketching, and folding origami renditions of them ever since.

Paper Suggestions:

Use back-coated washi, or colored art paper for this model. Use paper at least 10 inches square. Be sensitive to the qualities of the paper as you fold your turtle, letting it guide the style of your model, whether it results in a crisp, realistic, geometric model, or one much softer and more expressive.

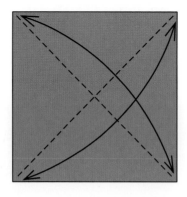

1. Begin right side up. Valley-fold in half diagonally both ways.

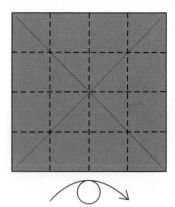

2. Valley-fold in half, edge to edge each way. One at a time, fold each edge in to the center and unfold. Your paper will be divided into sixteen equal squares. Turn over.

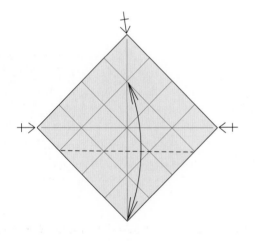

3. Valley-fold the bottom corner up to the top intersection of creases. Unfold. Repeat with the remaining corners.

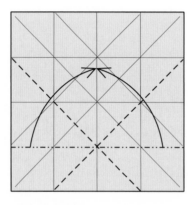

4. Inside-reverse fold the left and right halves of the bottom edge.

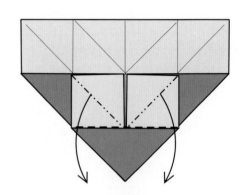

5. Squash-fold.

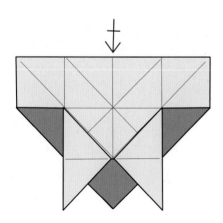

6. Repeat steps four and five.

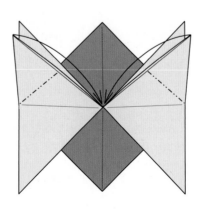

7. Squash-fold the center corners.

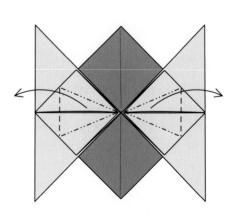

8. Petal-fold.

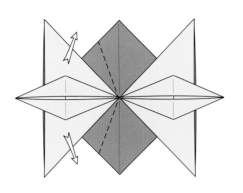

9. Pull the layers open.

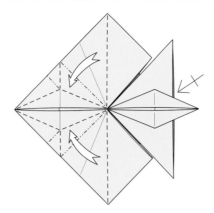

10. Follow the crease pattern to collapse the paper. Repeat on the other side. Look ahead at figure eleven to see how the layers should be organized.

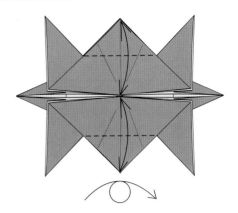

11. Valley-fold the top and bottom corners to the center. Unfold. Turn over.

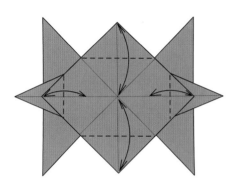

12. Fold the indicated corners in. Unfold.

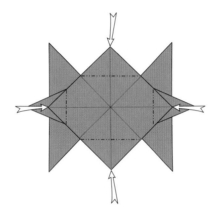

13. Sink the four corners.

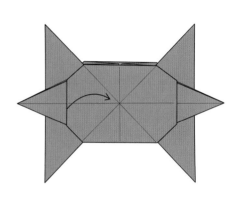

14. Move the top layer of the left side over. Avoid making a crease if you can.

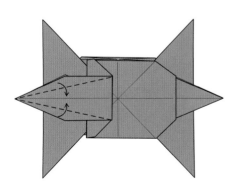

15. Valley-fold the edges of the tail paper to make it narrow.

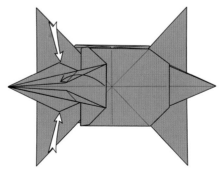

16. Sink the indicated corners of the tail paper. Move the top layer back to the left.

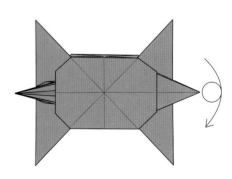

17. Turn over, top to bottom.

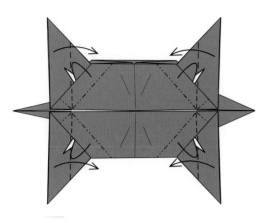

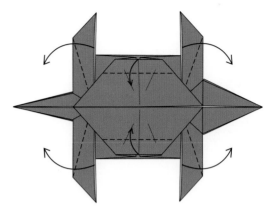

18. Mountain-fold the indicated edges behind the top layer, while folding over the paper for the limbs. Look ahead at figure nineteen for the shape.

19. Valley-fold the limb corners out. Valley-fold the indicated edges, squash-folding the accompanying layers that will follow. Look ahead at figure twenty for the proportion and angles of the folds.

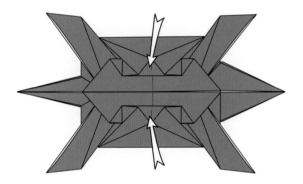

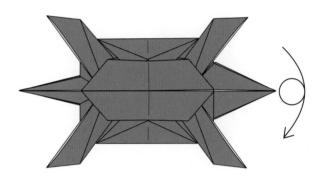

20. Sink-fold.

21. Turn over, top to bottom.

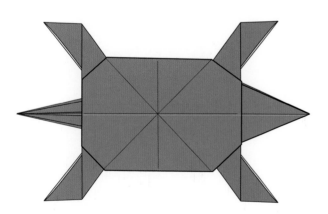

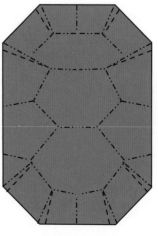

22. My pond turtle base. Many forms and details are possible. We will explore one basic development from here.

23. Pinch mountain-folds in the top layer of the shell to resemble a typical pattern of the major scutes, which are displayed on the shell of a typical fresh water turtle. Notice the crimps at the top and bottom corners. These will make the shell rather dome-shaped.

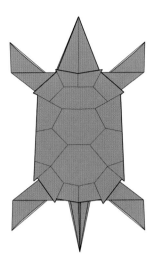

24. Here is the result of the crease pattern. It can be made to appear geometrically perfect, or loose and lyrical.

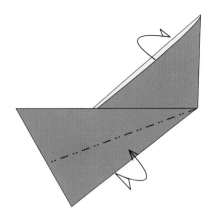

25. Begin to shape the legs by mountain-folding the leg in half and opening the corner to form a foot.

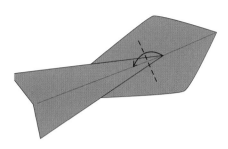

26. Valley-fold the apex back, where the foot and leg meet.

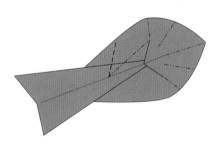

27. Crimp to form any bends in the legs. Pinch in mountain-folds to make the toes.

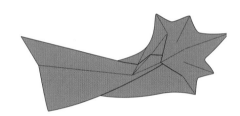

28. A leg and foot might look like this. You can vary the style and complexity as you like. Look at photos of live turtles to get some ideas of pose and gesture.

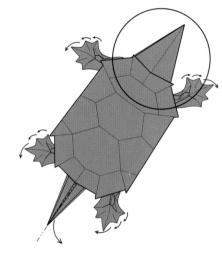

29. Curve the claws outward.

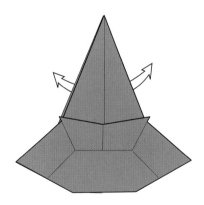

30. Pull open the layers of paper in the area of the head, circled in step 29.

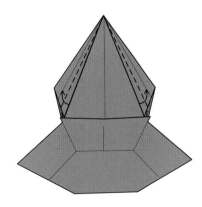

31. Notice that some layers are not opened. Valley-fold to make an extra overlap along the side of the head.

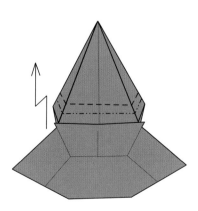

32. Mountain and valley-fold the base of the head to form the overlapping "turtle neck."

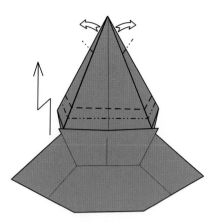

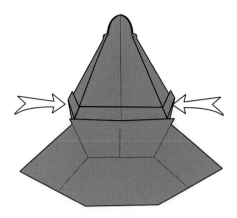

33. Open and round the end of the head. Pinch mountain-folds for the beak.

34. Close the neck and head.

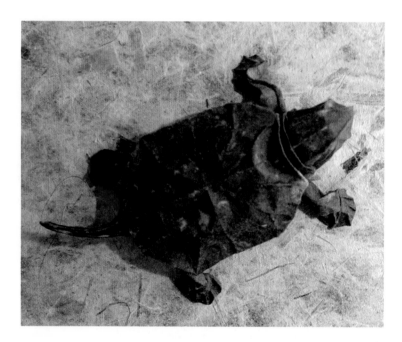

35. The Pond Turtle.

MUDARRI LUNA MOTH

Designed by Michael G. LaFosse

Michael has named many of his butterfly and moth designs for people that have inspired or helped him through the years. Greg Mudarri is a graphics professional and origami student and enthusiast. Greg designed the layout of the LaFosse Butterfly System book, Origami Butterflies. The Luna Moth is an exquisite creature. The vibrant color and slender hind wings seem much too showy for an animal that is active only at night.

Paper Suggestions:

I prefer to use maroon and pastel green duo washi for this model, but feel free to be creative with the color combinations you choose. Use paper at least 10 inches square.

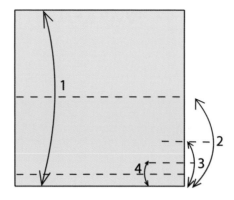

1. Begin with the paper right side up. (1) Valley-fold in half, bottom to top. (2) Make a short valley crease to mark the distance half way from the bottom edge to the valley crease above. (3) Make a short valley crease to mark the distance half way from the bottom edge to the new valley crease. (4) Valley-fold the bottom edge up to the lowest valley crease. Unfold.

2. Valley-fold the bottom two corners to the bottom valley crease. Use the bottom valley crease to fold the bottom edge up.

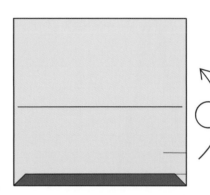

3. Turn over, bottom to top.

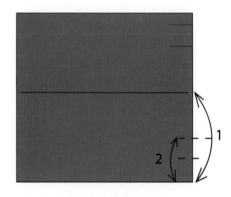

4. The folded edge should be at the top. (1) Make a short valley crease to mark the distance half way from the bottom edge to the valley crease above. (2) Make a short valley crease to mark the distance half way from the bottom edge to the new valley crease.

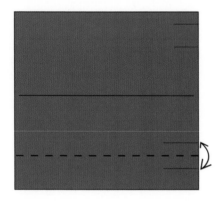

5. Valley-fold the bottom folded edge up, matching the two short valley creases. Unfold.

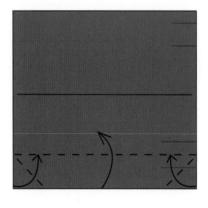

6. Valley-fold the bottom two corners to the full-length valley crease. Use the full-length valley crease to fold the bottom edge up.

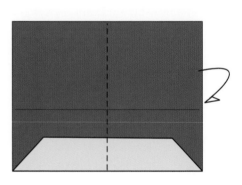

7. Mountain-fold in half.

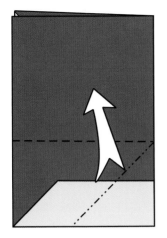

8. Squash-fold.

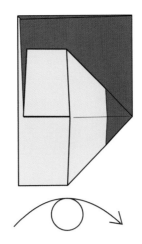

9. Turn over.

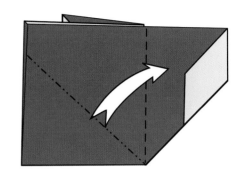

10. Squash fold.

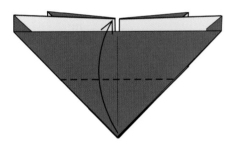

11. Valley-fold the bottom corner up to the top of the split.

12. Turn over top to bottom.

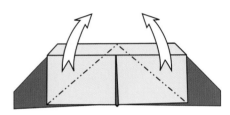

13. Squash-fold the wings up.

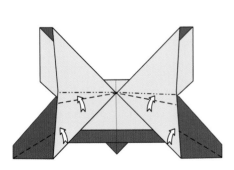

14. Crimp the middle of the top layer of each wing down, swiveling the leading edge of the hind wing up and stopping at the outer corner.

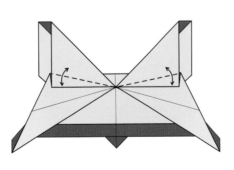

15. Valley-fold and unfold the middle folded edges.

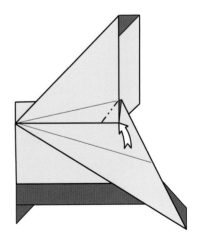

16. Inside-reverse fold the indicated corner into the wing area and up to the crease formed in step 15.

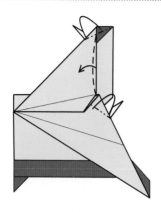

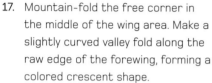

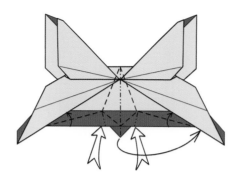

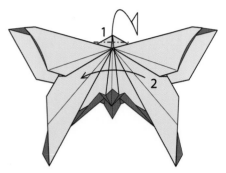

17. Mountain-fold the free corner in the middle of the wing area. Make a slightly curved valley fold along the raw edge of the forewing, forming a colored crescent shape.

18. Begin to form the body by mountain-folding the middle and then inside-reverse-folding the bottom edges up.

19. (1) Flatten and then mountain-fold the top corner for the head. (2) Bring the wings together with the body between.

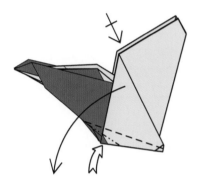

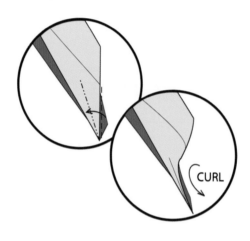

20. Narrow the back end of the abdomen with mountain folds. Fold the wings down on each side.

21. Valley-fold the exposed triangle of paper over the tail end of the hind wing. Gently curl the tail end of the wing.

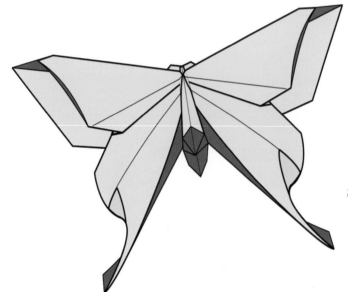

22. The Mudarri Luna Moth.

Designed by Michael G. LaFosse

Michael has been designing and folding orchids since the early 1970s, and has designed several that begin with a two by one rectangle. This design lends itself quite well to display in a cluster. Even though they are fast to fold, they hold their own when placed beside his more elaborate and showy individual orchid designs, such as his origami Cattleya Orchid shown in the Advanced Origami *book (Tuttle). The German TV series* In Search of Intelligent Life on Planet Earth *came to Haverhill in 2006 to videotape a segment at the Origamido Studio, specifically asking us to make a huge sheet of handmade paper. Since the show was to be seen on television, the director asked us to make a bright color, and suggested that we make purple paper. After the film crew left, there we were with a large vat of purple pulp, and a huge sheet of purple paper. Not that many origami models require bright purple paper, but Michael folded a box full of these little orchid blossoms that we decided to assemble onto a branch for co-mounting with some colorful butterflies. The piece lay unfinished in the Studio for months as I kept changing the arrangement, looking for the right colors and styles of butterflies to complement the bright purple orchids. We finally had our answer when the Lalique Company (French art glass) commissioned 67 Alexander Swallowtail butterflies in handmade, fuchsia and black abaca papers. The resulting composition became one of the anchor pieces at the Peabody Essex Museum's Origami NOW! show.*

Paper Suggestions:

Use back-coated washi, or colored artist paper for this model. Use 2 x 4 or 3 x 6-inch rectangles.

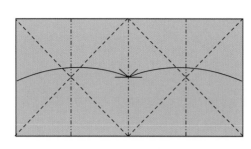 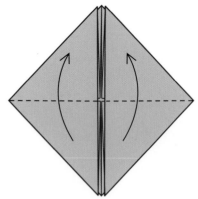

1. Mountain and valley-fold, as shown, and collapse the paper to resemble figure two.

2. Valley-fold the bottom two corners up.

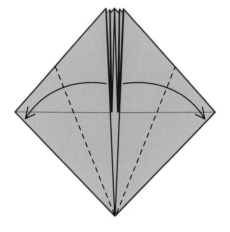 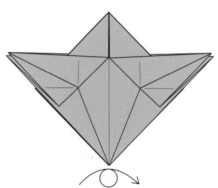 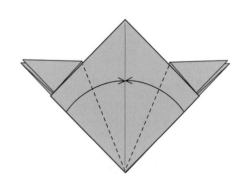

3. Valley-fold the entire set of center edges out to match the bottom left and right edges. Squash-fold the last layers to accommodate the final flattening.

4. Your paper should look like this. Turn over.

5. Valley-fold the bottom edges of the top layer to meet at the center.

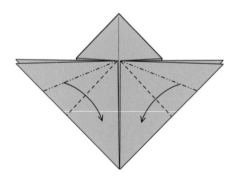 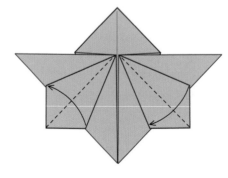 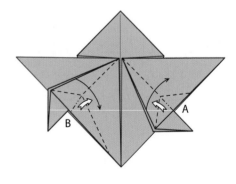

6. Squash-fold the top corners at the left and right, forming kite-shaped sepals.

7. Valley-fold each kite in half. Notice that the left side moves up and the right side moves down. A is the upper half of the kite and B the lower. They are folded differently from each other.

8. Inside-reverse fold and restore the kites. Notice that upper side A makes use of a symmetrical triangle form for the inside-reverse, while the lower B does not.

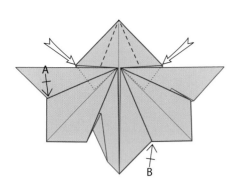

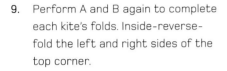

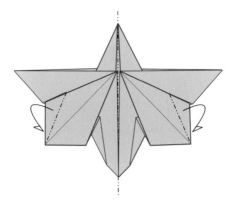

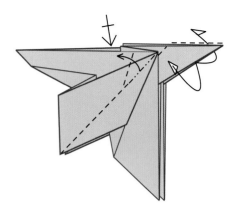

9. Perform A and B again to complete each kite's folds. Inside-reverse-fold the left and right sides of the top corner.

10. Mountain-fold the outer vertical edge of each kite to narrow the shape. Mountain-fold the model in half.

11. Swivel the indicated corner at the middle of the top edge of the model. Valley-fold the sepal in half. Repeat behind. Outside-reverse-fold the point at the top right.

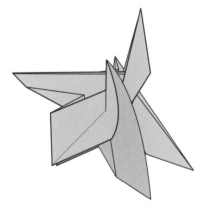

12. Your paper should look like this.

13. Open the paper edges in the center of lower petal and push in the back layer to form the lip.

14. The Munich Orchid.

Now create the orchid leaves.

ORCHID LEAF

There is no substitute for actually spending time with live orchids, observing, if not growing them yourself. The paper leaves should evoke the same rounded, succulent aspects of real orchid leaves.

Paper Suggestions:

Use back-coated, green washi or colored art paper for this model. Use a range of papers from 6 to 12 inches square.

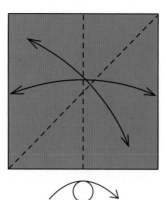

1. Valley-fold in half edge-to-edge once and diagonally once. Turn over.

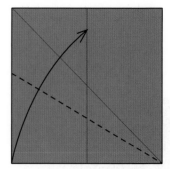

2. Be sure that the crease pattern is oriented as shown in figure two. Valley-fold the bottom left corner up to touch the vertical center crease.

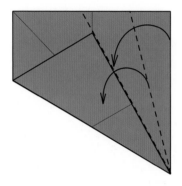

3. Fold the flap over and over twice.

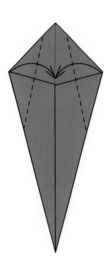

4. Fold the left and right corners of the kite shape to meet at the center as shown. You can make the edges parallel or angled.

5. Mountain and valley-fold the bottom end of the leaf to give it a graceful 3-D shape. Turn over.

6. The finished leaf. Refer to the Building Flowers and Plants section of the Techniques chapter for details on floral origami model construction.

F–14 TOMCAT FIGHTER JET

Designed by Michael G. LaFosse

Michael's first origami designs were paper airplanes, and this was the first model Michael published as Aero-gami. It was also the first of his models that I videotaped to prove the point to Michael that video was a useful tool for teaching origami: After looking at the drawings and shaking my head, I mounted a videocamera above Michael's folding table, and videotaped him folding the model. Without looking at the footage, I rewound the tape and loaned it to a neighbor with an 8-year old boy. Not only was he successful learning the model at his own pace, using Pause and Play buttons on the videocassette player, he proceeded to take more origami lessons from us! While trying to perfect the origami penguin, Michael came up with the base that transformed into this fighter jet. He had been impressed by the plane when it was released as a plastic hobby model in the local toy shop. He drew the diagrams with pen and ink, and lettered the instructions with a Kroy™ ribbon presstype machine. The booklets were featured in an ad he placed in Popular Science Magazine, and photocopies circulated throughout Air Force bases. We still hear from pilots and Air Force personnel about their experience folding and flying the F-14 Aero-gami model that Michael published in 1984.

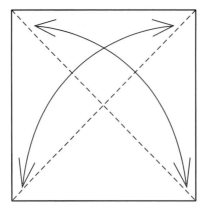

1. Valley-fold in half diagonally both ways.

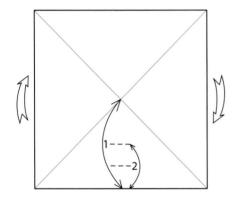

2. (1) Move the bottom edge to the center of the paper and make a pinch mark. Unfold. (2) Move the bottom edge to the pinch mark and make a new pinch mark. Rotate the paper so that the pinch marks are on the left.

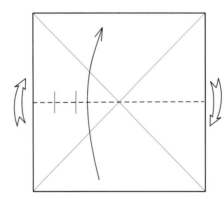

3. Valley-fold in half, bottom to top. Rotate the paper so that the folded edge is on the left.

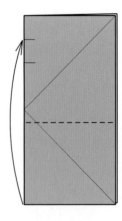

4. Valley-fold the bottom edge up to the top pinch mark.

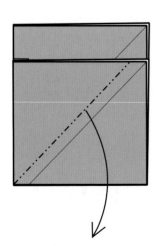

5. Squash-fold.

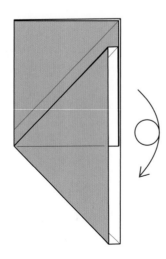

6. Turn over, top to bottom.

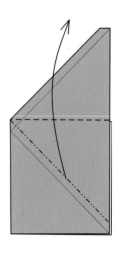

7. Squash-fold.

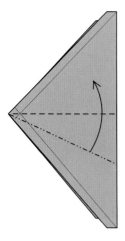

8. Squash-fold.

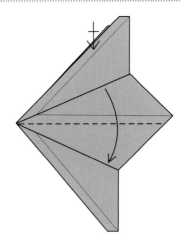

9. Fold flap down and squash-fold the upper half. Repeat 8 and 9 on the top flap.

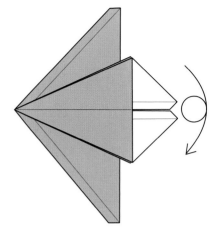

10. Your paper should look like this. Turn over, top to bottom.

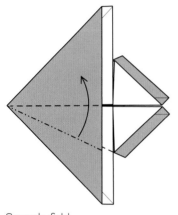

11. Squash-fold.

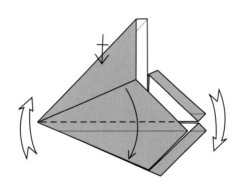

12. Fold flap down and squash-fold the upper half. Rotate the paper to resemble figure 13.

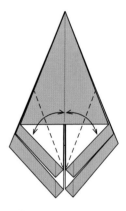

13. Valley-fold the indicated edges to the center. Unfold.

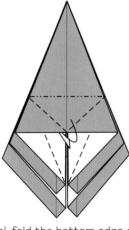

14. Petal-fold the bottom edge of the triangle layer inside the model.

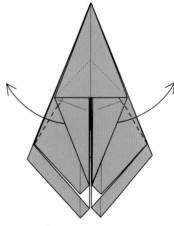

15. Inside-reverse fold the wings out. Notice the fine dotted line, which is an X-ray view of the petal fold inside. The innermost end of the leading edge of the wings should meet at the apex of the petal fold.

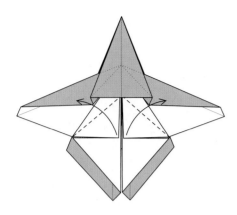

16. Valley-fold the two square corners out. Notice the limit set by the bottom edge of the triangle layer at the top.

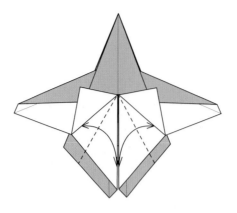

17. Valley-fold to match the middle folded edges to the outer folded edges. Unfold.

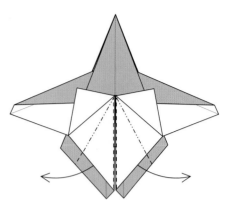

18. Inside-reverse-fold these two flaps.

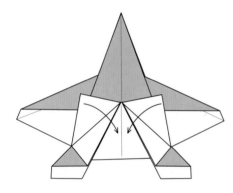

19. Return the square corners to their original place.

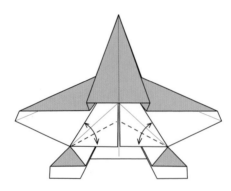

20. Valley-fold the bottom edge of each of the two triangles up to match the indicated crease. Unfold.

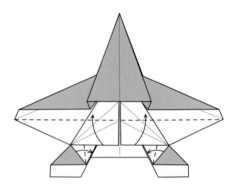

21. Valley-fold the bottom edge of each wing up. Squash-fold the accompanying layers that will follow the paper.

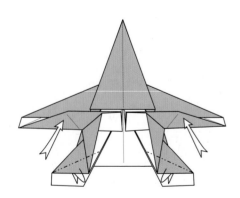

22. Tuck these edges under the front edge of the wings. Mountain-fold the free edge of the tail wings inside.

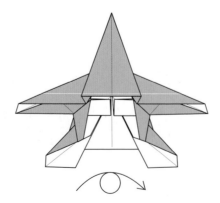

23. Turn over.

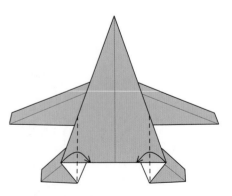

24. Valley-fold the left and right corners toward the middle and place them on the horizontal edge.

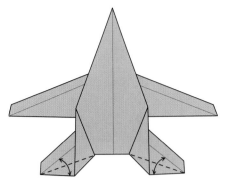

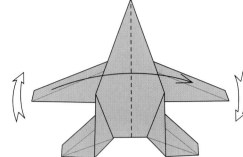

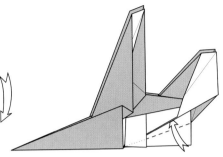

25. Valley-fold the bottom edge of the tail wings to the crease. Unfold.

26. Valley-fold in half, wing to wing. Rotate the model to resemble figure twenty-seven.

27. Tuck the back corner under the flap.

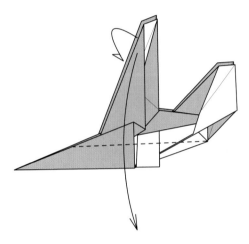

28. Fold the wings and fuselage center down to the sides.

29. Set the wings and vertical stabilizers as shown.

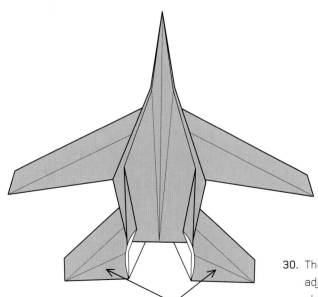

Elevator Flaps

30. The F-14 Tomcat Fighter Jet. Note that flight adjustment can be made by positioning the elevator flaps up or down.

AMERICAN ALLIGATOR

Designed by Michael G. LaFosse

Don't try this at home! (Just kidding!) One of our most prized origami models by Eric Joisel is his African Pangolin. We knew that Eric spent a whole week performing meticulous box-pleats in a logarithmic progression. We never imagined that we would be folding something comparable, not once, but twice. The Morikami Museum and Japanese Gardens in Delray Beach, Florida was the first venue for an origami exhibition called FLorigami. No show of Everglades animals and plants would be complete without an American Alligator, and Michael obliged. We missed the model so much we made another! This is one of those models that Michael pictured vividly in his mind, completely folded and finished, before he ever touched a sheet of paper.

Paper Suggestions:

Use back-coated washi for this model. Use paper at least 6 feet square. We recommend building up the large sheet from smaller sheets of high quality washi. Brush on acrylic color pigments, and let them dry. Re-moisten, then lay out and paste the overlapped sheets with archival polyvinylacetate (PVA) on a plastic drop cloth. Make two of these. Let them dry completely, then re-wet and bond them together with methyl cellulose or wheat starch paste, without worrying about the placement of the seams. They shouldn't show in the finished model, due to the extensive pre-pleating.

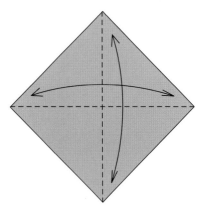

1. Fold in half diagonally, both ways.

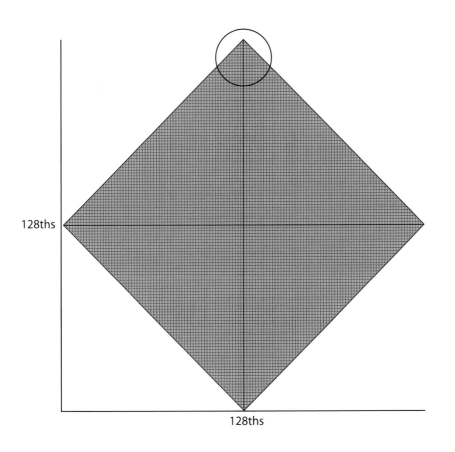

128ths

128ths

2. Fold into 128ths diagonally, both ways. Divide each major division in half: Two segments become four, then eight, sixteen, thirty-two, sixty-four, then one hundred twenty-eight! A long, straight bar of wood or metal, such as a T-square, is useful to fold against.

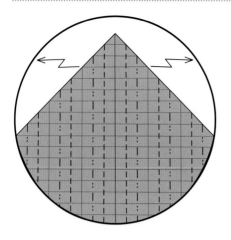

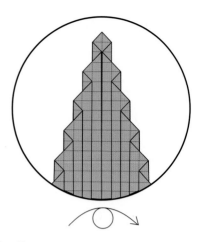

3. Mountain and valley-fold from the center out, forming a series of overlapping layers.

This photo shows the progress of this pleating.

4. Turn over.

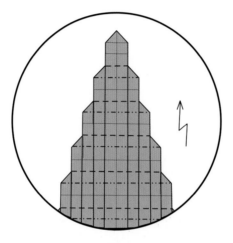

5. Mountain and valley-fold from top to bottom.

Here is the result.

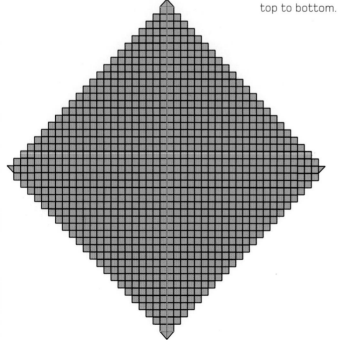

6. The pleated square is now ready to develop into the alligator. Notice that the pleated form may not be perfectly symmetrical. This is not a problem since the folding of the base is rather simple. Diagrams 7 through 29 will demonstrate the folding of this base. The scales have not been added for the sake of clarity. You should practice folding the base in ordinary, un-pleated paper before attempting the real thing.

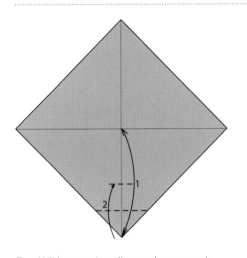

7. With crossing diagonal creases in place (1) move the bottom corner up to the center and make a pinch mark. Unfold. (2) Valley-fold the bottom corner to the pinch mark.

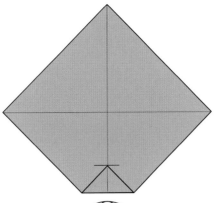

8. Turn over.

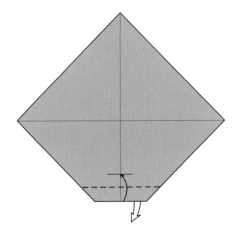

9. Valley-fold the bottom edge to the pinch mark. Allow the hidden corner to come from behind.

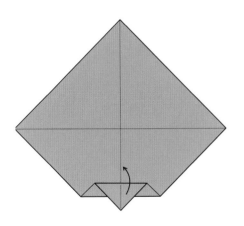

10. Unfold the corner up.

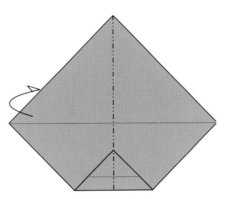

11. Mountain-fold in half.

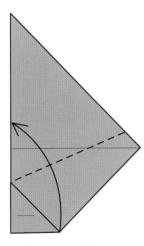

12. Move the indicated bottom corner up to touch the left side folded edge. Valley-fold from the top corner of the triangle layer out to the right edge.

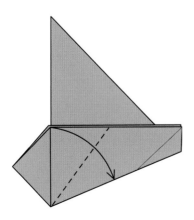

13. Valley-fold. Note that the hypotenuse edge of the triangle aligns with the bottom edge.

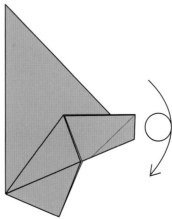

14. Turn over.

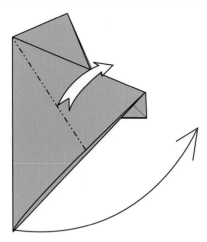

15. Squash-fold.

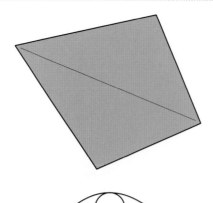

16. Turn over.

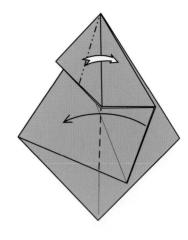

17. Squash-fold the top corner and move the indicated layer to the left.

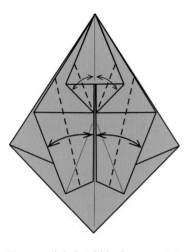

18. Your model should look symmetrical, like this. Valley-fold the indicated edges to the center. Unfold.

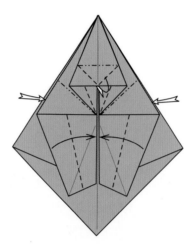

19. Inside-reverse-fold the left and right flaps. Petal-fold the bottom edge of the top triangular layer inside the model.

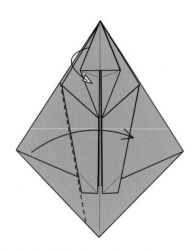

20. Pull out the loose layers from behind the uppermost shape. Valley-fold the left side over the inner left edge.

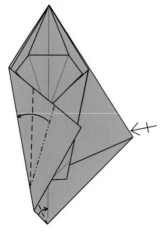

21. Crimp the left side to swivel it into alignment with the center. Notice the small valley-fold at the bottom corner. Repeat on the right.

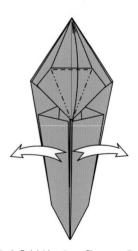

22. Petal-fold the top flap up. Pull open the side crimps.

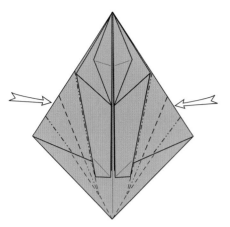

23. Inside-reverse fold the left and right sides.

24. Your model should look like this. Fold the top, rhombus-shaped area in half, to the left.

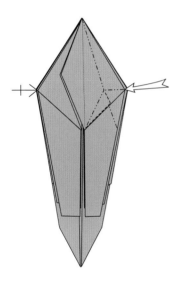

25. Sink this corner. Repeat on the left.

26. Inside-reverse-fold the four corners for the limbs.

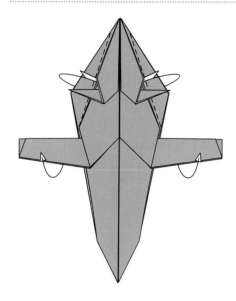

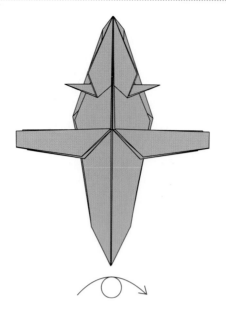

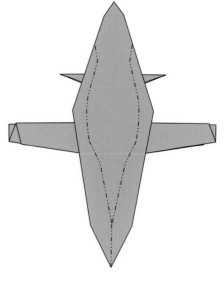

27. Valley-fold the left and right sides of the head and body in and under the front leg layers. Move the inside layer of the hind legs to the outside.

28. Your paper will look like this. Turn over.

29. The completed alligator base (good for any species of crocodilian). The following photos will be used to complete the demonstration.

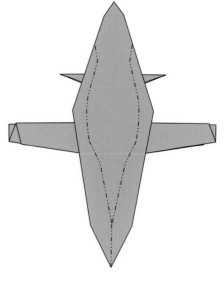

Mountain-fold the end of the tail in half. Form two mountain-folds, diverging up the tail and either side of the body. Contour the general shape of the tail, body and head.

30. Use tweezers to pull up and shape the tail scales that outline the top edge of the tail.

31. A bamboo skewer works as well. Shape each scale to add texture over the whole of the back.

32. Pull up a scale for each of the two eyes. It is helpful to look at a photo of an alligator's head to approximate their location on the model. Pull out the leading edges of the front corner to widen the area of the head. Pull scales out from along the edges of the upper jaw for the teeth. Form the teeth by folding the edges of these scales inward, making them sharply pointed.

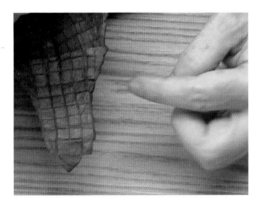

33. Here is a view of the lower jaw, which can be found beneath the head corner. Pull scales out from along the edge of the lower jaw for the teeth. Form the teeth by folding the top edge of each scale over, forming a point.

34. Shape the lower jaw and set it into position, open and below the head. The outside edges of the lower jaw should be folded upward so that the teeth point up.

35. Refine the shape of the head and add the nostrils. You can insert the tip of a skewer behind a scale, lifting it and forming a rounded edge, implying a nostril.

36. Restrain the neck and jaw with a strip of cloth, tied around the neck. Remove when completely dry.

37. With the neck and jaw secured, begin to shape the joints of the legs. Use softly rounded bends at the shoulders, elbows and knees. Let the thickness of the accumulated layers of paper imply powerful muscles here.

38. Close-up of a knee and ankle.

39. Use the many-layered pleats to form the webbed toes by splaying them open. Refine the ends of the toes with sharp folds for the claws.

40. The American Alligator.

THE ORIGAMI ART PROFESSION

By Richard Alexander

INTELLECTUAL PROPERTY

There are some origami models that have been around so long that nobody can recall who designed them. We call these "Traditional" models, and they are available to the public for fair use without royalty. The classic Japanese crane is one example. There is another category of simple origami models that are derivative from common bases and traditional models. The origami community is infused with a sense of sharing the empowerment of folding paper, especially with youngsters. Lillian Oppenheimer, founder of the Origami Center of America and an excellent teacher, encouraged creators to be generous with their creations and folding technologies. This does not mean you are allowed to publish or use other people's origami designs without their permission, or without giving them due credit as the designer or creator.

Michael has been diligent in respecting the intellectual property rights of other creators, and we have maintained an extensive library of hundreds of published origami books for reference, should any questions arise. We make our living by creating new origami models, and using those creations to make props for photography, videography, tangible advertising and window displays. We develop folding methods that are fun, unique, and often set to the patter of an entertaining story or rhyme. We consider our designs and folding sequences to be our intellectual property, and often give permission to others to use these rights for their own personal use. We charge a fee for others to use these properties for commercial purposes.

Other people involved in creating, teaching or performing origami for a living should also develop a plan to diligently respect the intellectual property rights of other artists who have gone before them. This includes preventing the unlawful copying and "sharing" of published books, photos, images, diagrams, stories, audio and video files, as well as conscientiously compensating the creators, many of whom depend upon those funds for their existence.

It is troubling that while we and several other professional artists make our living by creating origami that is new, fresh, and fun to fold, there seem to be some people out to capitalize on the illegal sale or use of these creative, intellectual properties. It is up to the community of origami creators, therefore, to appropriately shun those who do not respect the intellectual property rights of the legitimate creators. If you are making money on origami that is not traditional, or not your own design, be sure to first obtain written permission from the author, and don't forget to give compensation and credit to whom it is due. Not to do so could expose you to the action of lawyers, and wrath of millions of Internet Savvy origami enthusiasts.

The best protection for your original origami design work is for you to do thorough research and to document your designs by publishing them on the web or in print. Keep written records of all contracts and permission grants that you issue. If you discover that someone is representing your original design without your permission, contact the offender in writing immediately. Document all developments. If satisfaction is not forthcoming you should consider retaining the services of a lawyer who specializes in copyright and intellectual property issues. Origami creators can band together to address Internet infringement in a cooperative way, by pooling their resources with larger corporate sponsors, such as publishing and cable companies, to go after the thieves.

DEVELOPING YOUR MARKET

When we started the Origamido Studio, we listed several general categories of products and services that we anticipated developing. We had no idea who would call. We had no idea who else would develop competing services.

Many of our customers turned out to be involved in home schooling. Many families were actively looking for fun things for their members, often from three different generations, to enjoy together. Neighbors that enjoyed the company of others found that origami walk-in classes brought them together with those who enjoyed using their hands to make things of beauty and wonder. We tried not to be an origami production house that cranked out thousands of commodity objects. For instance, rather than fold 1,000 cranes for somebody's bat mitzvah, we encouraged the celebrant to bring her friends to a class to learn how to do it themselves.

If you are determined to explore a career as an origami artist, start by searching the Internet. See what others are offering and charging. Dip your toes into the business by starting with a small website. Offer only what you know you do well. The response—feedback, orders, and repeat business—will help you be sure your abilities and services are in demand before you commit more serious sums of money to the venture. If you are offering origami jewelry, greeting cards, or even pieces for tangible advertising, be sure that the models are your own design, or from the recognized traditional repertoire, or folded only under written terms of permission and license from the author. It is customary for people who fold the designs of others to send a royalty check to the author on a regular basis, according to the terms of the written agreement. It is also important to attach a card to each piece, identifying both the original designer and the folder.

Perhaps the best advice about developing a market for origami art and services is to do enough different things that none of them become a chore. Teaching origami in elementary schools or dealing with commercial art or publishing deadlines can become onerous. Making art solely to others' specifications ceases to be art. When these tasks are mixed into the schedule,

each in moderation, the artist has a better chance of staying balanced, fresh and upbeat.

The good news is that there appears to be no limit to the type of origami art-related business you can start. Whether your strength is in performing, teaching, fashion, window design, public art, advertising, entertaining, interior decorating, marketing, illustration, packaging design, or all of the above, you are limited only by your creativity and drive. Get some real projects under your belt, document everything, then show prospective clients what you have done.

DESIGNING ON DEADLINE

The creative process is difficult to push. On the other hand, nothing motivates better than a big check payable to you, and a deadline. Before offering to complete a task, be sure you have the abilities and capabilities—to a point. Artists who do not stretch beyond their comfort zones do not grow as artists. Origami is such a unique art that there are relatively few accomplished practitioners to offer an alternative at a lower price. As soon as they do, move on. You will have found the right market when you can design on deadline, make a profit, and feel good about the product. When your customer agrees, you have at least one repeat customer. Do this for a number of years, and you have a career doing something you love.

QUESTIONS TO ASK WHEN OFFERED A COMMISSION

More important than finding the right vocation is finding the right customers. There are so many potential customers for origami art, teaching or advertising services that few will truly understand the limitations of the art, the intellectual property constraints, or the demands on you, the practitioner. Commissions represent shared visions. You must probe your customer's mind enough to envision exactly what they expect you to deliver. There are so many choices that unless they are ordering from a catalog of your work, you had better be sure you have sufficient artistic latitude to please them. If you flip through your catalog or brag books and they seem quite particular about their likes, and approve of only of one or two things you have done before, perhaps you will not be able to please them. If on the other hand, the client likes everything you have done for others, no problem! If you decide that this customer can indeed be delighted with your work, here are a few items you should discuss before committing yourself by taking a deposit.

Scheduling

- When is the final art due? These deadlines may be hard or soft. A hard deadline is a serious commitment. If your art is not ready for presentation at the Awards Banquet, you will not be paid, and your reputation as an artist who can deliver the goods will take a serious blow. A soft deadline may be for a casual gift, such as a housewarming, that may not be tied to a specific date.

- What amount of time is allowed for concept development? Will the customer need to see the work in progress, to confirm size, color, pose, or to make decisions about framing, a pedestal or mounting?

- Will you need to hear from more than one person about the production schedule? (You may be working with several people, such as an events coordinator, communications director, or marketing manager, and each may have their own different deadlines.)

Budget

- How much money are you entitled receive? When will you receive it?

- What are the terms? Our commissions require a 50% deposit. Will you receive the rest of your money upon their receipt of the art? Will they send you a check in 30 days? Some companies and most government projects take much longer to pay their contractors. Get the terms in writing, and be sure you state that you will charge interest for the amount not paid when it is due.

- For large, corporate projects, have you budgeted a contingency sum to cover unforeseen additions? There are often reasonable requests for re-working a concept or producing additional units.

Rights

- Who will have ownership of rights to any and all original art? If they take photos of the art, will your name be listed as the artist? If they reproduce the image for other items, such as calendars, coffee mugs, or bookmarks, will they credit you? Will they pay you?

Limitations

- Is the customer considering concepts other than origami? You must be comfortable with the client's understanding of origami's limitations. Chances are good that they have no idea how much time it takes to design and fold an origami model. One client requested that we design and build a working Ferris wheel… until we gave them the estimate.

DOWNTIME

It is easy to spend every waking moment developing your business—working on the next book, design or project. Human beings need rest, and some of the success of the Origamido Studio has been that I kept a full time job during more than half of our time on Wingate Street. Working with youngsters making paper airplanes in the evenings was a perfect antidote to dealing with difficult legal issues in my consulting business. We sensed that Michael also needed time to explore completely different interests, and he has earned his second degree black belt in Tae Kwon Do, purchased a new flute, and was regularly attending the local seashell club.

INSPIRATION

Artists need inspiration. The minds of creative artists seem to feed on stimulation, whether nourished by travel to strange new places, or journeys to the inner thoughts of the mind. Perhaps time spent contemplating the works of nature, or just discussing issues with friends and acquaintances will be enough to fuel the creative impulse. One of the other artists on Wingate Street would visit area museums with other artists and friends nearly every Friday. It is important for people to travel, experience different cultures, ecological biomes and their creatures.

That's one of the reasons why we're so excited about our upcoming move to Hawaii. We can't wait to develop folding patterns for the colorful fish, tropical birds and exotic creatures that exist only there. Stay tuned!

RESOURCES

SUPPLIES

Carriage House Paper
245 Kent Ave.
Brooklyn, NY 11211
Phone: (800) 669-8781
www.carriagehousepaper.com

Papermaking supplies, handmade papers & Methyl Cellulose

Hiromi Paper International
2525 Michigan Ave. Unit G-9
Santa Monica, CA 90404
Phone: (310) 998-0098
www.hiromipaper.com

Washi, Papermaking supplies, handmade papers & Methyl Cellulose

The Paper Connection International, LLC
166 Doyle Ave.
Providence, RI 02906
www.paperconnection.com

Wholesale source for Washi and more

Twin Rocker Handmade Paper
100 East Third St.
Brookston, IN 47923
Phone: (800) 757-8946
www.twinrocker.com

Papermaking supplies, handmade papers & Methyl Cellulose

University Products
Phone: (800) 628-1912
www.universityproducts.com

Abaca Tissue, Natural Washi and Methyl Cellulose

ORIGAMI

British Origami Society
www.britishorigami.info

Not for profit organization dedicated to serving the needs of the origami community, worldwide. Membership includes magazine subscription. Hosts two annual origami conventions.

Gallery Origami House
www.origamihouse.jp

Makoto Yamaguchi's design and publishing house of complex and super-complex origami books.

Japan Origami Academic Society
www.origami.gr.jp

One of Japan's top origami associations of complex and super-complex designers. Membership includes magazine subscription. Hosts an incredible annual origami convention.

Joseph Wu's Origami Page
www.origami.as

One of the most complete link resources for origami on the Internet.

Origamido
www.origamido.com

Website for the origami art of Michael G. LaFosse and Richard L. Alexander.

Origami On Demand
www.origamiondemand.com

Downloadable video lessons for beginners.

OrigamiUSA
15 West 77 Street
New York, NY 10024-5192
Phone: (212) 769-5635
www.origami-usa.org

Not for profit organization dedicated to serving the needs of the origami community, worldwide. Membership includes magazine subscription. Hosts one of the best annual origami conventions in the world.

ACKNOWLEDGMENTS

We are grateful to Edward Walters and Tuttle Publishing for making this book possible. It is indeed a privilege to be offered such a quality venue. We are especially indebted to our editor, Jon Steever, whose careful work and guidance has helped us through the many challenges of organization and on to completion.

The Origamido Studio would not have happened without the inspiration of Akira Yoshizawa's pioneering work in origami art, and the early, loving support for origami enthusiasts in the USA provided by Lillian Oppenheimer.

We could not have developed such a meaningful relationship with Master Yoshizawa were it not for Emiko Kruckner, who accompanied Michael to Japan, and Mr. and Mrs. Yoshizawa to the Peabody Essex Museum, several years before the Origami NOW! show materialized. Then, only a few people recognized origami art for its significance.

We also acknowledge the extraordinary work of Makoto Yamaguchi and his staff at Gallery Origami House in Tokyo for their support of talented young origami designers around the world. Mr. Yamaguchi has been especially helpful in making it possible for these young artists to attend foreign conventions, and to take advantage of internships at OrigamiUSA, and the Origamido Studio.

Several advanced designers, including Robert Lang, Daniel Robinson, and Satoshi Kamiya, worked with us to develop special, handmade origami paper blends, and without them, the art would not be where it is today.

It is amazing to realize that exhibitions of fine origami art did not exist just a few decades ago. We are indebted to the tireless pioneers who brought this work to the public, at a time when doing so was not easy: Robert Cates (Yamawaki Center), V'Ann Cornelius (Mingei Museum), Eric Joisel (Carousel du Louvre), Reiko Nishioka (Morikami Museum and Japanese Gardens), Tom Wallman (Hangar 7), Jonathan Baxter (Southeast Origami Festivals), Kristina Durosier (Fitchburg Art Museum), Joseph Wu and the Directors of OrigamiUSA (PCOC-Vancouver), Jane Winchell, and Ellen Soares (Peabody Essex Museum).

We are indebted to the LaFosse and Alexander families, who missed us at many functions during the decade of our operating a retail store, and whose support helped us to continue through the rough times.

Finally, we have been inspired by so many wonderful mentors, colleagues, associates and students, we would be remiss if we did not mention at least some of their names: Anne LaVin, Jan Polish, Jean Baden-Gillette, Sok Song, Jill Bellwood, Jean Spires, Andrew and Chris Bell, Tiffany Paquette, The Roderick (Rocky) Cumming family, John and Kim Benner, David Brill, Kenneth Baclawski, Alice Gray, Alexander Soukas, Doris Asano, Laura-Lee Hayes, Florence Temko, Anthony Matosich, Orit and Adam Goldstein, Karla & Graham Cook, Joyce and Bethel Saler, Zeljko Rabidic, Rico Mochizuki, The Robert Rossi family, Heather Gavin, Charles Yee, The Koretsky family, Chris K. Palmer, Tom Hull, Kunihiko Kasahara, Joan Salas, Erik and Martin Demaine, Randall Yaw, Patti Grodner, Ben Mueller, Nathan Geller, Seth Friedman, Jeannine Moseley, Gay Merrill Gross, Tomoko Fuse, Theresa-Marie Brown, Paulo Basceta, Roberto Gretta, John Scarborough, Michael Manheim, Leo Shapiro, Philip Yee, Ethan Plaut, Elsa Chen, Christine Clement, Matthew Gardiner, Gary Chin, Bryan Chan, John Montroll, Jeremy Shafer, Marsha Dupre, James Puccio, Linda Haltinner, Ashley and Diane Woodward, Greg Mudarri, The Friedstein Family, Sipho Mabona, Lauren Pearlman, Brian Rafanelli, Lisa Luchetti, Jason Ku, Hatori Koshiro, Ushio Ikegami, Maria Velasquez, Kyoko Kondo, Linda Chapman, Valerie Vann, Roz Joyce, Tony Chen, Valerie and Chris Ellis, Cory Comenitz, Rob Hudson, Rob Weinstock, J.C. Nolan, Marcia Miller, and all of the supportive teachers, librarians and students, as well as our countless beginning origami students and friendly customers of the Origamido Studio.

This book is dedicated to the advanced students, colleagues, and collaborators at the Origamido Studio. For over two decades, we have enjoyed making handmade paper and folding origami art with them in Haverhill, Massachusetts. Dozens of advanced students have wet-folded colorful koi fish at our home on the banks of the Merrimack River, or made handmade paper with us during the ten years that our Studio was located downtown on Wingate Street. These thousands of hours of working and folding together helped crystallize our thoughts about exquisite origami art, and certainly helped to usher in a new era of appreciation for professional origami art installations and exhibits around the world.

DISTRIBUTED BY

North America, Latin America & Europe
Tuttle Publishing
364 Innovation Drive
North Clarendon, VT 05759-9436
Tel: (802) 773-8930
Fax: (802) 773-6993
info@tuttlepublishing.com
www.tuttlepublishing.com

Japan
Tuttle Publishing
Yaekari Building, 3rd Floor
5-4-12 Ōsaki
Shinagawa-ku
Tokyo 141 0032
Tel: (03) 5437-0171
Fax: (03) 5437-0755
tuttle-sales@gol.com

Asia Pacific
Berkeley Books Pte. Ltd.
61 Tai Seng Avenue #02-12
Singapore 534167
Tel: (65) 6280-1330
Fax: (65) 6280-6290
inquiries@periplus.com.sg
www.periplus.com

First published in 2008 by Tuttle Publishing, an imprint of Periplus Editions (HK) Ltd., with editorial offices at 364 Innovation Drive, North Clarendon, Vermont 05759.

Copyright © 2008 Michael G. LaFosse

Library of Congress Cataloging-in-Publication Data

LaFosse, Michael G.
  Origami art : fifteen exquisite folded paper designs from the Origamido Studio / Michael G. LaFosse, Richard L. Alexander.
      p. cm.
  Includes bibliographical references and index.
  ISBN 978-4-8053-0998-8 (hardcover : alk. paper)
I. Origami. I. Alexander, Richard L., 1953- II. Origamido Studio. III. Title.
  TT870.L234255 2008
  736'.982--dc22

                        2008015258

Printed in Singapore

PHOTO CREDITS

Photography by Michael G. LaFosse includes: Akira Yoshizawa with Origami Gorilla, abaca paper sample, Banana Slug, Modular Flower and Leaf, American Alligator, and Saks Fifth Avenue commissioned window displays including Summer Flowers, Butterflies and Tulips, Halloween, and Silver and Black Leaves with Hyperbolic Torch.

Photography by Greg Mudarri includes: Traditional Japanese Ceremonial Noshi, Traditional Origami Japanese Crane, Traditional Senbazuru of Three Connected Cranes, and Richard Alexander's Class at the Origami Studio.

Photograph of Richard Alexander's Paper People by David Bradley Photography, S. Boston. Courtesy of Trinity Communications, Smart Pages.

Photograph of Pegasus commissioned window display for Hermes of Paris by Richard Cadan.

Photograph of the Puffer Fish by Sipho Mabona.

Photograph of Michael LaFosse's Class at the Origami Studio by Jane Winchell.

Photograph of Alexander Aztec Swallowtails on Purple Munich Orchid by Dennis Helmar, Courtesy of the Peabody Essex Museum.

Photograph of the Peabody Essex Museum on pages 60 and 61 ©2008 Peabody Essex Museum. Photograph by Walter Silver.

All other photography by Richard L. Alexander.

ABOUT THE AUTHORS

RICHARD L. ALEXANDER holds a B.S. from Cornell University, where he studied systems biology (computer modeling of nutrient and energy flow through ecosystems) as well as landscape architecture design, art and visual communications.

As a Certified Hazardous Materials Manager (CHMM), he has been an environmental programs manager, consultant, workbook author, videographer, and an industrial trainer since 1975, specializing in chemical handling, hazardous waste management, wastewater treatment, aquaculture systems design, and ISO14001-the international standard for certifying environmental management systems in government and industry.

With Michael LaFosse, he co-founded Origamido Studio in 1996, a commercial design studio, hand papermaking facility, classroom, and fine art gallery. Alexander has designed dozens of origami models for beginning and intermediate level paper folders, and has taught hundreds of origami classes at the Origamido Studio. A pioneer in video origami instruction, he has produced LaFosse's extensive series of private origami lessons on video since 1992. Alexander has authored *LaFosse's Origami Butterflies: A Field of Discovery Through a System of Design* (Origamido, Inc.). He has personally made much of the handmade Origamido™ paper featured in the works of dozens of origami masters, and has designed several origami commercial and fine art exhibitions.

Origamido Studio's commercial clients include: Saks Fifth Avenue, Hermes of Paris, United Nations' UNICEF, Lotus Development, Columbo Yogurt, Reebok-Rockport Shoes, Pfizer Pharmaceuticals, Union Camp Paper (IP), Corbis Insurance, McDonald's Restaurants, NASA, QVC, Talbot's, ToySmart, Fidelity Capital, Creo, General Motors, Unica, Ian's Natural Foods, Comcast, Lalique, and several events planning, print and TV advertising, and print publishing companies.

MICHAEL G. LaFOSSE, best known as a hand paper maker and paper folding artist, has been practicing the art of Origami for over forty years, and teaching it for over thirty years.

LaFosse's most popular works in handmade paper are natural history subjects.

In college, he studied biology at the University of Tampa. He returned to Florida to study the animals and plants of the Everglades for origami art designs, and has created spectacular shows of folded, handmade paper sculptures, not only in Florida at the Morikami Museum and Japanese Gardens, but also at the Arizona-Sonora Desert Museum in Tucson, where over 40,000 people saw the works. LaFosse's works have also been shown at the Carousel du Louvre, Paris; the Peabody Essex Museum in Salem, Massachusetts; Hangar 7 in Salzburg, Austria; and at the Fitchburg Art Museum. Photographs of many of his pieces from those shows are in his hardcover books, *Paper Art: The Art of Sculpting in Paper*, ORIGAMIDO: *Masterworks of Folded Paper*, *Advanced Origami: An Artist's Guide to Performances in Paper*, and in several other self-published books and DVDs. LaFosse is the host for origami and paper airplane folding on Comcast On Demand's Activity TV™, series for kids.

• • •

Michael G. LaFosse and Richard L. Alexander have produced approximately five dozen publications. They have hundreds of thousands of students all over the world learning origami from their books, kits, DVD video lessons, computer downloads, and now on cable On Demand programs.